Prodigy:

Ayanna Lea

Scripture taken from the Amplified Bible, Copyright © 1954, 1958, 1962, 1964, 1965, 1987 by The Lockman Foundation. Used by permission. Used by permission. www.lockman.org

Prodigy Copyright © 2021 by Ayanna Tipton

Published By: You Can Make It Books, LLC
www.youcanmakeitbooks.com

ISBN: 978-1-7366651-2-1

This is my dedication: To Eagle Doves

Eagle Dove; What's love?

My children saying hello to above;

Giving; Eagles hugs.

Eagle Dove; What's love?

Seeing beauty for ashes; speaking hope to cores within.

Eagle Dove; What's love?

Having a Dr. Oscar J. Nelson Dowdell-Underwood.

Speak life with Heavenly insight.

Eagle Dove; What's love?

A Jill on a hea'l.

Eagle Dove; What's love?

Food being prepared out of pure love;

Mama's Boy Catering LLC.: Malcom, brother hugs.

Eagle Dove; What's love?

Your sister owning your story making room for Glory.

My Eagle Dove; Dr. Tish's love.

"You can make it," that's true enough!

Eagle Doves: this is my dedication to Grace's, undeserving;

unconditional love.

Letter to Senior: DB

My love is full capacity. It was my anger that fought me. I have to say thank you because like pastor, you had hope for me. You preached order and the importance of a plan. You called your son daily; trying to encourage a praying man. I think about your life and the fight you won. Here you are today, standing like a soldier that fought and won. Survivor holding Guns. Heavy weight champion: I know one.

Letter to Naomi:

Like Ruth with no fruit, my dirt trail leads me your way. It was rough, but tough created a diamond in a rough. Showing a second to son.... created a father to my daughter to sons. A gem... a prodigal son. I thank you for your love that traces back to the cornerstone; showing why honoring mother's is important to daughters to sons. I love your grace walk; and face talks.... even behind walks. Being part of your life cost. I had to let ill thoughts fall off. I am here today to embrace the time that I thought was lost. 2012: remember love began and was never lost. Like Ruth with no fruit... My dirt trail leads me your way. It was God that kept light and the days... when it was hard to pray. To Marie of more...a heart I am thankful for.

Table of Content

I am **A Y A N N A L E A**

I am the choice that chose Truth.

I am the flower that once produced weeds.

I am the Life that suicidal thoughts tried to deny.

I am the virtuous woman that once was sexually immoral.

I am the meek spirit that could not control her temperament.

I am the prodigy of Grace manifestation. I am **A Y A N N A L E A.**

The Prodigy: Summary

If only a girl knew that God places Heavenly angels in sight of spiritual blues. It is not just your fight; but we are in this too. I was scared to write this book; turning something old; into new. Even more, how could I tell my story without telling yours too. Just speaking truths. I am no longer lame. I am healed brand new. "Rise up and walk." yeah you! This little girl that always cried blues. My momma wasn't... My daddy didn't... She did, He did... I want... I cannot. Booooooooooo! A little girl that never wanted to accept her gift; but rejected... so; my life reflected. Looking for love in all, but the One. Life beat me until God's truth became sum. It was hard for me to love and forget... that later turned into a pool, full of regret. Trust who? Not you! Forgive? Just die so I can live. I will never forget what you did. "But you have to, so you can be your true you." Faith over fear... Hold on? 28 years... true story. I tell myself, do not look back if you cannot praise and clap...yes reflect on your story. To God be the glory. He carried me through the pains to write this story. I have learned to fly, instead of weep with no hope and cry. I learned there's wounded eyes' fried; but if I tell my story.... maybe they have a reason to push; keep going and survive. It is God's Grace why I am still alive. You know how many times I told myself; I am finished and ready to die. I am still standing... what looked like an end; I saw a hand. He pulled me up, gave me strength and called me a friend. Jesus is the reason for this story. He intercedes for me; now Father God wants my story. Told the world to see; that it was not me; but He, that helped me write this story. If only a girl knew that God places Heavenly angels in sight of spiritual blues. It is not just your fight; but we are in this too. I was scared to write this book; turning something old; into new. Even more, how could I tell my story without telling yours too.

Thank, Yanna! I love you Yanna

A Note to my children:

My mom was a street walker. My mother gave me up for adoption. My adopted mother, I love dearly. She taught me cleanliness and godliness. She was very stern. My foster mom told me something that made me no longer believe in her love: "You're going to be just like your mom." Mommy then ran away at sixteen and got pregnant with Rasheed. I was living with his father, and we ended up in Chicago. Rasheed's dad got locked up and I kept running away. Finally reached the family support center where the troubled youth were. Afterwards, I received a probation officer because I kept running away. I ran away because when the woman I loved told me I was going to be just like my mom. I told her, "I might be." … It made me feel like she did not love me, so I did not want to be there. She wounded me deeply. Then I met your dad when I was 17. Rasheed was three weeks newborn. I walked past Our House Restaurant, your grandmother's restaurant. I begin working there. That was my first job.

And the rest was history. I forgive your dad for beating and abusing me; but I will never forget the hell he put me through. Mommy always loved you all. Mommy wants you to know that I was still with you, though I was far away. I loved all my babies. God kept me strong to come to this point today. I am able to communicate with you all and get to know each of you. I am thanking God for that! I uphold myself through God and his strength to carry me all through my turmoil and strife. So, I am here today thanking God: and all I can do is give him the glory, and the honor, and praise, that I am able to speak with every last one of you all, and to see you all achieve your goals. And I love you all that is all.

Some of my fears are losing one of you all; or getting killed and hurt.... And I do not want that. I try to reach out to every one of you all. Each of you are my babies and I just want to know where you all are and for you all to know where I am. I just fear not having you all in my life because I did not have that...... I did not have a mother or a father. "Real mother or father and you all have both! It is only one par....and I would have cherished it if I had that bond with you all. I do not understand agony, evil, mad, and strife. ... you know. Just get over it and grow up; and love one another. This is a new beginning. This is a time where we need to all reach out to one another, instead of being elementary...... It is unnecessary. It is time to grow up and be mature minded about things in a positive state. The negative stuff can stay away. I love me for my strive and faith... for never giving up.

I did drugs to numb my heart so I couldn't feel the deep wounding. Doing drugs made express myself. It gave me courage to speak out. I was timid without the use of drugs. Drugs enhanced my mental thought; and I often had to deal with the consequences. But... Mommy is still here. The true story comes to light every time. The truth is the truth!

I am that scale; if it ain't leveled out or equally yoked, I cannot do it. I pray for it until it gets together and when it's one accord, I'm good with it. I learned to forgive and move on. It is not easy to forget; but now I just keep it moving. I walk by faith and not by site. God has been answering every prayer that I ask for and it is so amazing. I be like wow. All of you all start calling and coming around…. And this is what I needed in my life to bring joy, so I can see my grandkids grow up.

My real parents… I did not have that Yanna. So, you know. That alone was it for me. There is nothing like your real parents. Even though I loved my adopted parents, it still is never the same. When I saw mixed parents, I would be like dang… this is how we would have been. I would just sit back and stare at them. Lol they be like why is she staring at us like that. The only reason why I was staring because that was something, I wished I had.

I loved my mother on the strength of having me. She did not have to have me. I give her love and honor on that part. She gave me to a family that can love and provide for me. … and the needs she could not. All I can say is God bless her and I hope to see her again in life. I hope to lay eyes on my real dad, even if I do not talk to him. I just want to look at him and say, that is him. My dad asked my mom to not mess up his marriage and family he already had, and she honored that and moved on. I was the prodigy of that.

Marjorie Martiz Massey (Tipton)

Voice typed and approved on March 6th of 2021

Though words could never explain the way I feel. How I could ever forget vivid memories of a dark childhood that once was my present. The countless tears rushing down my face are stained on my wounded heart. I still daydream of the nightmares haunted by your controlling corrupted mentality. Sometimes even just a little sun through the weary rain calmed the storm, me and my siblings experienced. Though I grew to understand the tough love you gave, your bad will never outweigh the hell you put us through. I learned to forgive you a long-time age. I despised the way you dogged my mother. I hated the man I was supposed to learn and look up to all my life. The womanizer in you created a mannish deceptive state of mind inside of me. I never knew personally what it truly meant to love or be loved. I was forced to grow up fast watching my dreams be unwillingly taken away from me. I became a ward of the state. Though I was quiet as a child my soul cried for help. My heart grew cold, and my anger got out of control. Crazy thing is you taught me about God through all your demons you yourself we are dealing with. I loved going to school and the morning yet; I dreaded coming home. I ran away from home, but I could not run away from the pain that ate at me like cancer. What did not kill me made me stronger. Everyday my life is a challenge thirty-years later… Because of these vivid memories I still deal with my past; but today I stand like a warrior with my head held high covered in GOD'S GRACE…I will perfect my purpose…Signed Rasheed Massey

When I was young, I felt like the black sheep. I thought I was never good enough. My father had it out of me and I never knew why. He always told me I was stupid dumb and retarded. And all types of stuff; knowing I felt every word. When my brothers and sisters did things that he did not approve of, he automatically assumed I did it; because I was the oldest; out of the last four of my dad's children. My father was supposed to be my teacher and the person I could talk to; but I never got that. So, I turned to the streets. My mother on the other hand left in the mid 90s because of my abusive father. He beat her when I was in her stomach which caused me to be premature. My mother did not raise us, we raised ourselves because she was in the streets addicted to drugs, and prostitution. With that being said, I had no one to talk to that could help. I wanted to talk to my dad's mom before she passed; but I did not want my father to beat me for talking to her. So, I grew up rejecting authority and not listening to people. I ended up stuck in the system. Now that I am in my 30s, I have yet to talk to my father about my issues; because I witnessed my sister try and do the same; only to get shut down and cussed out. So, I just kept everything to myself and asked God to give me wisdom; because if I do not deal with what is

on my heart and mind, I will never get to tell my father how he made me feel now that he has bone cancer.

As of now, I came across a blessing. Someone I can talk to. That understands everything that I am going through and loves me unconditionally. She is my rock. She is holding me up, when I am down and out and feel like everyone is against me. I am planning on giving her my last name, but it is crazy because I hate my name, me and my father has the same name. And I want to know why I was always beat on and looked down upon. I need closure with my father. I want him to know how I feel. I want to introduce him to my wife; but I do not think that is a good idea. It is a love, hate relationship between us. But I am alright.

All the love that I was looking for is in one person, I never felt it, so I cherish every moment with her. And it is crazy because she is in Illinois and my father is in Illinois. And I am living down here, and I do not know where he is at. And I am cool with that, because I have a new family that loves me more than the family I got. Am I wrong for that? She wants me to connect with my father, what would I look like telling her no."

-- Jeffrey Lee (Massey) Tipton

To my siblings:

I have carried the weights of all of you all's pains. It was my hope and dream since I was a little girl for me to be in one room with ALL my siblings: with expressions of love. I dreamed of us all growing up together, living under a healthy roof. It brought me great joy pretending that we were all healed and free from our wounds. Dion; Aisha, Lamonica, Christina, Christian, Jeffrey, Jared, Tranitra, (Ayanna; ME); and now, baby Eli Jeffrey.

All our mothers were beautiful spirits inside out: Ms. Theresa; Momma Ruth, Ms. Sheila, Marcia (Mommy)... (Unknown). Mothers, I want to apologize to each of you publicly, for the strength of my dad. My dad treated each of you horribly; leaving each of you wounded, hurt, and confused. I pray that you all forgive him and find rest in Jesus. Know that my heart bare witness to the pain each of you endured. I love each of you beautiful spirits dearly. Each of you have shown what perseverance looks like. I am forever grateful for the enlighten smiles that each of you offered when I was in all of you all's presence. Momma Ruth, all those days you cooked that good food; yes ma'am; elated. Mommy all those times you nursed yourself back to life and gave strength; forever thankful. GRATITUDE. Ms. Theresa seeing you pop in the shop getting your hair done by the abuser sister and still engaging in family functions; Yes, Ma'am I remember: STRENGTH. Ms. Sheila, your kind understanding heart of gold. You are a precious jewel. I am forever thankful for our conversation in the summer of 2017. God has not failed us yet. I hope this book finds a place in each of you all home to heart. Let us all remember Ephesians 4:31-32.

Ephesians 4: 31-32 AMPC

³¹ Let all bitterness and indignation *and* wrath (passion, rage, bad temper) and resentment (anger, animosity) and quarreling (brawling, clamor, contention) and slander (evil-speaking, abusive or blasphemous language) be banished from you, with all malice (spite, ill will, or baseness of any kind). And become useful *and* helpful *and* kind to one another, tenderhearted (compassionate, understanding, loving-hearted), forgiving one another [readily and freely], as God in Christ forgave you.

Love Again

I know what voided love feels like. Love without holding contemp. Love through hate. Love, without feelings and emotions. Love. Love. Love! I say, when envy is the display. Love without carnal gain. Love. Love. Love. The color of flowers knows love. Love Dove; Peace now and forever; again: Love, loves: Win Again.

Prodigy is a WHOLE chapter within itself. It took strength, hope, faith, love…. obedience and sacrifice. Please note any curse words used in this book is to give depth to the intensity of conversations wrapped in feelings and emotions from various persons. The few curse words listed were the norm.

…. We acknowledge, then we forgive. We operate out of love and truth. Welcome to New Beginnings.

OXYGEN

What is life if you cannot trust the trees to bring oxygen?

How can one say they are living if they never perished?

What is knowledge if wisdom was never thought the right way?

Is your living in vain?

One of the common things that we as humans struggle with is whether our lives have purpose. Was everything that we have encountered in life a mistake, accidental or intentional? I was no exception to this questioning. Feelings of abandonment have pained me throughout my life, followed by undesirable defeat. These emotions left me with an emptiness. I did not understand the importance of living. Many of my life experiences have exposed oppression.

The numbness of reality made life hard to reason with. These early hurts in life set the stage for several emotional wounds as an adult. Was abandonment, feelings of being unwanted, pools of pain, no joy, no peace, to be my legacy in life? No, but it took years for this reality to manifest.

I had no consistent peace. There was always a need of light to break the clouds of darkness. There was always a need to clothe the cold. Boiling hot water in sets of seasons was deemed the norm. Watching street walkers get the credibility of "being," and or existing," made me discredit my own value in society. I often questioned myself, wondering where my belongings and purpose rested. I wonder why it was so easy for strangers to receive attention and affection that I longed for.

There were nights where I could not sleep due to the loud music being amplified throughout the house; on to the neighborhood; along with misbehaviors; resulting in full blown abuse. In addition, there were marking evidence of bullets hitting our home on different occasions. Busted heads from being pistol whipped. Men circling my dad in the entry way of our home at gunpoint taking his jewelry. I also recall ducking in pops car in order to leave off the Winthrop. My siblings and I could not lift here heads until we were at least three blocks out.

Winthrop was a five-story home with great potential. However, pops thought he cold finish the many undone projects he created. If one had to use the restroom, we had to usher them to the one upstairs: the bathroom in the basement was horrific, with layers of scum and no proper drainage; the restroom on the main floor almost never worked... we had to "Nigga-Rig" it for it to work and the stink produce no water ... and the times it did, left standing water; lastly, the bathroom on the third floor... whew. One could see through the floor, exposing the pipes and themselves. If one were on the main floor and come through the front door and kept straight; they could have very well saw whoever was in the restroom at the time. That sink also did not work. The knobs to the tub were wrenched.

The kitchen had broken marble floors: cabins with no doors, fire stains on the wood, plastic over the door and windows, the oven was rigged as well, turning the eye temperature was done with tools; the sink drained into a tall steal pot. We often had to take the top and dump it into the dysfunctional restroom next to it that usually had an odor.

The pantry is where we kept the dishes and food. Beans were always found no matter if we had food that day or not. The refrigerator was just nasty to say the lease. Blood from meant sitting in the bottom, rotten foods; etc. However, I would clean it and steal a few lemons cookies out of the 24 pack; also sneak a drink of grape soda. I was terrified to get caught; but it took hours usually for an approval.

I remember it being normal for my siblings and I to sit in front on my dad's locked bedroom door and bang on the door for hours pleading for food; meanwhile, he had his share in the room with steak and potatoes. If dad did answer, he blamed the children (us) for not un-thawing the half of cow he purchased that was froze improperly. My siblings and I ate Rally's more than anything; and on occasions we dined in at Ryan's, because pops didn't feel like cooking.

Now when pops cooked, the man could burn... literally. Sometimes he'll forget the food; but when he didn't his fish was excellent, and salmon patties, and cornbread. I hated the boiled chicken and canned mixed vegetables. Pop's sweet potato pie was in excellence; but my big brother Jared cooked it best. He taught me how to make something out of nothing.

In life, as children, we compare life situations to our own perception of what living truly is. Sometimes we are left with no comparisons of how to perceive excellence because our minds focus on the physical; rather than the up right spiritual. Children often go by what they see and hear. The trauma of hearing abuse, rather: physical or verbal caused my insides to shut down. I then learned fear, and this followed me into my adult years.

Being housed with a multitude of demons was the concept of bondage. When the furnace would sound without producing heat and the cold wood floors would squeak without a trace of a human life; those sounds made me fearful. Later, that awkward cracking sounds matched figurines. I saw maybe three total and felt one in the presence while I kneeled to pray in the upper room.

"I remember getting out of my bed to pray; and a dark cloud came over me. I wanted to jump back in the bed, but I was too scared to do that even. As I closed my eyes, to pray; I felt something on my back. Talking about fear…. I was terrified." From that day I stopped kneeling to pray, and I also stopped closing my eyes. I needed to see…. But seeing did not help! It paralyzed my vision. I believed in the physical. Seeing beyond my physical eyesight; confused my inner peace.

Dungeon Safe

Where dungeons stay;

 they lay.

Creating no room for safe.

I'm crying…

Graves replying;

"Come. Stay."

"Let me go!"

But where to escape?

Fear built a wall inside of me. All of us have fears, some greater than others. I was fearful of the very man that was raising me. I never knew if the day would expose brokenness and lack of control. Now grantee all days weren't bad, but from day to day you never knew if the house would be deemed peaceful or hells gate. The atmosphere could shift in a blink of an eye. "Who drank my damn pop! I know I had more than this left! Who ate my damn cookies?" After the roll call, we all knew it was beating time. I never got beat personally, but my brothers endured greatly.

Shattered fragments scattered into every aspect of my life. Red nights, full of crimson blood splattered memories of defeat. Defeat was a common feeling I endured. Anxiety was my response to life. The torturous cries of fear and pain from my siblings; and the cries from broken women that lacked true identity of self, destroyed my core. I wanted to help; but how?

My view of church and God became a major struggle as I watched: suits get pressed, shoes shined, and strings to instruments tightened, haircut crisp and dyed, chaotic words being expressed due to rushed disorder…. to pulling into the parking lot at church; and later watching pops fall asleep next to his guitar; only to ask us what we learned after church, as if he was woke.

Church wasn't anything pleasant for me. I usually went in with an attitude and was ready to roll my eyes at anyone that stared too hard in my direction. I was embarrassed I must say. I was usually stuck in disgust and jaded ill will. I wanted my clothes to be fresh. I wanted to sport expensive perfume; but it was me sitting in old dingy hand-me-downs making the best out

22

of what I had. More times than not; folk wanted to get close enough to me to get some insight on my life with no effort to help. I was silenced with dysfunction. I was accustomed to the various faces of dysfunction: yelling, cursing, fighting, hurt, and blame. As a result, I lived my life centered on confusion. Pain wove the fibers of my being.

Seeing women come and go and not one of them being my mother caused seeds of disrespect to grow. As women pranced into the backdrop of my life, I was getting numb. I never talked about my mom nor her condition. I just wanted to be where she was. Years of missing my mother was painful. I didn't feel normal. I was embarrassed by the thought of someone asking about my mom; let alone my dad. That seed grew into a plant of weeds; but all along, I was the flower that would one day spring.

How many nights have you cried yourself to sleep? How many lies did you believe, telling you that you were alone? This is how I felt numerous times throughout my life, but God has ever forgotten me, nor forsaken me. My secret petitions of my heart were to be free, to live without fear, and to experience something different than the abuse, neglect, and abandonment I endured. Many times, it is hard for us as individuals to recognize blessings in the midst of traumatic life situations.

Wings

To Testify truth being easy would be considered a lie.

Butterflies don't start with wings to fly.

R'U

Who are you?

The U in the Who of being.

Chasing, Trapping Love, has been my thing.

Brokenness,

 tried to recreate and make me out a theme.

Life taking flight; I'm still hoping for that Dream.

Who are you?

I am,

The U in the Who of being.

As I reflect; I was constantly beating death's wings. Dressed in all white; didn't feel right. I received recognition with no vision. I needed validation to feel the competition of success. Ayanna Tipton: I hated my name. My name felt like a total mistake, embarrassment. Fifth grade graduation was like a funeral ceremony.

Graduation Defeat

"Where are the folks that birth me?

I know these people in this filled gym can see;

That Dry eye's is rooting deep pains inside.

Why me?!

I'm embarrassed! Hurt! Ashamed!

Everyone can see;

That it's only me…

Standing where my parents were supposed to be."

Without catching my breath, in sixth grade, I sang 'I Believe I Can Fly' by R. Kelly with a knot of caged times. The anointing covered the notes I didn't know I could reach. After I sang, the judge released us; giving us the notion that we were now free... but defeat still ate me.

I began cleaning, massaging, and saving lunch money; so, I wouldn't blend with poverty. I felt like no one cared. I had to work to feel like me: seeing value, quality; instead of surrounding defeat. I learned early, lazy feet don't eat. Though I held money; I'd steal food to keep. Now, I'll get gel and pads and make sure to make that last; but If I had, I'll bubble up tissue for pads.

Continuing sixth grade, two of my best friends passed away. It was a very confusing time. I hadn't realized that people of all ages could die. The tragedy struck me similar to my grandmother's death. I don't recall having much emotional display at the funeral. I was present in body, but mentally disconnected. I wanted to be at peace; my eyes were crying... but no tears of peace.

In the shifting time of my life, I had no one to talk to about my pains. At night, I sat in the stillness of love songs; waiting for an answer to fall in my lap and give me clarity. The more I reflected on life and the losses I had endured, the angrier I became. I struggled to understand and couldn't wrap my head around my life.

In seventh grade, my sister and I were pulled out of Short Ridge to attend Guion Creek Middle School. It was a short-lived transfer; only lasting about four weeks. The school discovered we lived on the northeast side of Indianapolis; we were forced to withdraw. My sister and I got to see the difference between public and township schools. They had way more resources than the public schools. Our backdrop from our previous schooling showed we were behind on the learning curve they had set. However, the short time at Guion, I felt more encouraged to push beyond my limitations. I also was able to take on the material being taught; math actually became my favorite subject.

I needed to see that someone cared and believed in me. While attending Guion, I felt like a student for the first time in forever. I felt like I had something to prove; and I did an excellent job proving myself, but that wasn't good enough. My sister and I returned to Short Ridge Middle School to complete the remainder of the year. I didn't give my best; no one seemed to care, and the work didn't push my brain. I did just enough to graduate to the next level.

Dying Feet

I feel like I am dying.

I can't catch my feet;

Just the pattern of defeat;

Unstable in the elements that's defying me.

Dying feet; dragging the I Am in me.

Broken Butterfly

... I was that bee that didn't sting,

Set apart different;

Better yet a caterpillar with broken wings.

I can't see my dreams.

I just wanna be sweet like honey;

Cuddled with affection, harmony, and money.

Broken butterfly...

I know you're a caterpillar,

But do you have colorful wings that extend and fly?

Broken butterfly, what's a moth...

I was told it was a royal cloth;

Emerging from a caterpillar,

Hanging upside down soft.

Broken beauty;

I know a caterpillar grows and flies; shedding silky cocoons,

turning into beautiful butterflies;

Sitting in the fields with natural beauty, holding flowers. Singing

daisy; tulips to life.

Broken butterfly, you're healed, Fly.

Chugging along into high school, locally known as Ripple, I was still battling with my identity. While still searching, I was growing and developing into my own little person. For the first time, I started seeing life as a game to be played. I figured out a system of how to master the perception of hiding who I truly was. I was blocking and shielding myself from confronting the truth.

During my high school days, I was not socially challenged. I had senior friends as a freshman. Most people found pleasure in my presence. Some days were better than others, I will admit. My attitude could turn cold with a matter of seconds. On my off days, I found myself in the principal's office. I dreaded getting in trouble, but once I figured I was already in trouble; my mouth got even more reckless. If I was going to get a whooping… make it count. More times than not; I'd be scared for nothing… pops didn't spank me. However, I wasn't a troubled student. I was having issues at home at times that carried over into the school day.

While attending high school, I repeated the same cycle that I had already learned and adapted to in elementary and middle school. I did just enough to get by, to maintain fair grades so that I could be part of dance and the cheer team. I loved cheering because it gave me something to look forward to. Cheering consumed the last part of my day, allowing me to spend less time at home.

I never paid attention to my surroundings. One night, after getting off the school bus from cheer practice, I couldn't get into the house. Later, after I learned that the back door was unlocked, I wanted to rip my heart out. Due to the lack of communication and structure, I was seconds away from becoming a rape victim. The fact that there were four children in the home; with me being the youngest, I never understood why we could not have the key to our home. We also had to share rooms in a five-story house; the girls confided to one bed and the boys to their own together.

Grace, favor, and mercy always knew me…...

The second half of ninth grade, I was pulled out of school due to another dysfunctional daily outbreak. Family complications were the norm for the clan. My sister and I moved and transferred to Brownsburg High School. During the stay, we danced with Images of the Light. Religion made me believe that dancing in the name of Jesus was honorable. I never understood where my heart should be, in order for my praise offering to move to a place of true worship. When I danced, I danced for me. I did not dance for God or to receive his glory. Dance was covering the voids of discomfort.

I always did okay adjusting to new atmospheres, in hopes that it would be a greater change than the previous ones. However, change was starting to become problematic to my state of security. I feared change. I was used to being moved and shifted around from years prior. This time when I relocated, I was looking for a stable environment to call home. However, within weeks we were back to where home was considered to be.

I then began to lose hope in others. I felt as if no one really cared about my being. I became very nonchalant. I did not care about too much. However, whenever I saw someone who I thought was stable, I would vent to them in hopes that they would help. I knew I needed some guidance; I didn't know who to lean on and where to start. I was careful about being exposed to the need because I had a great idea that the help would be temporary and leave me more broken than before the help received.

My sophomore year, I was back at Ripple. I rejoined the cheerleading team. Cheering allowed me to get closer to the game I loved: Basketball; plus, I could go to the games for free. Ripple had a winning team, which made cheering that much easier. One of the star players was Steven A. Jamison; and another starting five: Armond "Tre." Steven was a very gifted young man with NBA Dreams. In the middle of my sophomore year, I lost my sister. She was no longer living on with me. I never told anyone, but that killed me softly. I worried about her from the time she fought pops to the outside world of shaped freedom. While looking for a friend, I found one in Steven. Steve secured the spot temporarily.

During my junior year, Steven became noticeably ill. The illness was later identified as cancerous. He was no longer attending school. I hated my life at this point. Steven's sickness was a distraction to the Ripple community as well as to thousands of others. While Steve was fighting for his life, relationship wasn't the goal. I beat myself up for months after Steven passed, because I was too weak to stand with him. I didn't understand the person he became. He was usually the sweetest thing talking; and for him to turn sour; it broke my mental. I again had been let down.

Live Remark Break

From Friend to Brother: Armond Patterson

Growing up in my neighborhood (Fairfield), wasn't easy; but it definitely made me who I am. Luckily, I was always involved with sports. Basketball has always been a way for me to release some stress and to stay out of trouble. I have always been a star player on all of my teams growing up: from School 48, Shortridge, Ripple, and many others… AAU team's etc.

I played college basketball for 2 years at Hesston College in Kansas. I wasn't taking school serious and eventually I quit school. I went back home and began working different jobs. I began to realize that I wasn't meant to work the way I was.

I have always been a part of a team from paying basketball; so, I felt that I needed to do something else. I had a cousin that was in the Army. He educated me about the Army. So, I decided to join the Army as a: Pharmacy Tech. I have been in the army for 6 years now.

I always wonder what my boy Steven would think of me now. Steve was my best friend since the 8th grade. He was like an older brother to me. He always looked out for his friends and family. Our junior year at Ripple, he was diagnosed with colon cancer and it changed the whole environment. I had just seen him the day he had passed away. I was on my way to Florida for a basketball tournament; but before I left, I went to his house and talked to him. I tucked him into bed and told him I will see him when I get back. As soon as I landed in Florida, my phone was blowing up telling me that he passed. I literally couldn't believe it; because I had just been with him a few hours ago. Steven's death was the worst pain I ever had in life. I just always wonder how far he would've been in life.

Steven and Ayanna were dating for a while. Ayanna is like a sister to me. We've been knowing each other since kindergarten. We also lived 2 blocks away from each other. She is caring, selfless and fierce if need be… lol; but always been passionate about what she does. She was a cheerleader, dancer, beautician, cook, etc. I am proud of her and how she has overcome the obstacles in her life. Continue to be great and always know that I'm with you when you right, and Ima let you know when you wrong. Stay true to you because that's all you got. – Armond "Tre" Patterson

Before Steven passed, I started talking to this dude named Wesley. My best friend Cam introduced me to this dude. In May of 2010, I lost my virginity to Wesley prom night. As I reflect, I can't say it was rape or unwillingly… forced, maybe so. Any who, prior to losing my virginity; I was always scared to have sex. I feared my dad. However, admission was given, and my virginity was taken. I was terrified. I didn't know what to expect during and afterwards. Intercourse was a new adventure. All I wanted to do is dress up and feel beautiful for the entire night, as if it were my wedding day. I didn't want to have sex, but something in me desired the intimacy. I wanted to know if having sex would defuse past and present pains I was experiencing silently. Right after prom night; I broke up with Wesley, but he wouldn't leave me alone. I couldn't figure out why. I felt so trash for letting a dude I barely even knew touch me. Yes, he was fine; just not my type. Crazy part, I gave in and let him stay around me after the breakup. I enjoyed having him as an option. I then began dating an old crush Mo.

Cinderella

I'm beautiful only if time could see.

I rush seconds; with no peace.

Anxiety keeps finding er' way... back to me.

Sweet, calm…

That's what really shaped my inner me.

My eyes are more than what my soul keeps.

Cinderella you're a Queen to Lea.

You wear your crown and dust haters frown.

Cinderella! You're a jewel Easter found.

Cinderella. Cinderella. Cinderella.

Cinderella left in deaf ears,

It's Queen Easter tilting Crowns.

I do enjoy sweeping, but in my house now.

Feeding the flock with little to no moaning and growing sounds.

It's a pleasure delight. I'm really grateful that Cinderella found

joy and fight, in midnight.

In 2010, I was still running from things that were killing my insides. Mastering my true, authentic self was not desirable. Hiding the truth and not looking for solutions caused me to run deeper in the tunnel of crisis. Going to school in hopes that Steven would walk in one of our classes we had together was my main focus, not education itself. Steven never returned back to school. Junior year was my last year at Ripple. I was expelled for not following the rules and guidelines of the school community. I sat out of school for weeks. I later enrolled into Arsenal Tech, where I finished out my junior year. However, more than anything, I wanted to talk to Steven and make sure he was as comfortable as possible; but since it seemed as if I failed when I had the chance... I did not even bother him. Plus, I felt guilty for giving up what I thought belonged to him. However, the time I was reconnecting with Mo, Steven passed. Talking about closure; I had none.

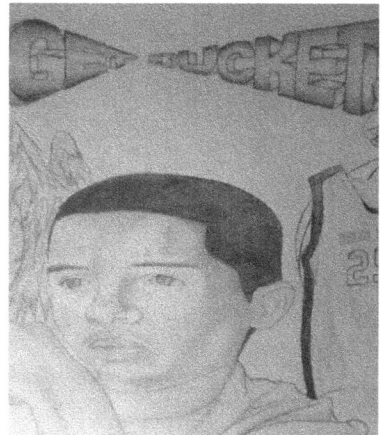

Steven passed away July 23rd, 2010. Steven's passing troubled my spirits. Suicidal thoughts took over my mind. The pain I felt, I just wanted to die already. Steve's death was the worst. I was at my darkest place after Steven passed away. I wouldn't eat, nor talk much: sipping on water and eating sour pouches... dassit. I would just cry in pain. I remember asking God to take my life. I saw death as an easy way out and a peaceful state of rest. I was tired of being left dealing with life's pain on my own. I sat in the second row at Steven's funeral and didn't move my eyes off the casket the entire service.

I was blocked out of life. The very person that gave me reason to look for the sun in each day had life taken from him… I didn't understand why he called Steven's number #25.

Every standing wall felt as if it was caving in. Anxiety filled my nerves. Worry kept me tossing and turning. Fear was crippling my heart. Anger set into my flesh and rooted through my body. My informalities awakened the evil in me. I grew to hate life in total. Within a few days of Steven's passing a train nearly ended my life; God kept me. I knew then I didn't want to go out like that. However, I still didn't want to be among the living… it was too painful to face my realities. Death seemed to shape peace.

As summer break was ending, I knew I had to shift again… Back to what home was considered to be: Fairfield and Winthrop. I was battling with even more personal issues than before. My mind was altered and uncensored. I was torn. I was only at peace knowing I was closer to Mo. I used Mo to try to fix my pain and discomfort and for a while it worked. Mo was a gentle spirit. He never reminded me why I wanted to die. He actually started being the reason I smiled again. I needed a distraction to refocus my thoughts and feelings.

In 2010, all my siblings were gone and had been for some time now. However, my "home" was now accompanied by a family of eight and their dog with fleas. I wanted to just throw the whole man away. It burned me seeing the man I wanted to show me love and affection; give it to others willingly… that made my heart burst in flames. Not to mention, some of her children share the same kin. How embarrassing was that! Humiliating. We even had bed bugs and roaches in the house now. That was my ticket out. One thing about me, I don't do filth. No matter where I am, I make the best out of it. I never knew that saying, "Goodnight don't let the bedbug bite," was true; until then.

February 4th of 2011, I moved from Winthrop and in with Mo and his family. I cried to Mo about my current living situation and how life treated me prior to him. No matter the dysfunction, Mo showed he wanted to stand in the gap of my pain. Mo was my best friend. Though Mo wanted to be my support system he couldn't. I soon left after understanding that I can't play house. I brought a high level of sin in his home. Ms. Veal never put me out; my pride and insecurities led me out of her home. I could not handle the pressure of being obedient and taking instructions. I wasn't used to parental guidance.

I left Mo's home after I found my mother in the streets. For some odd reason, I was so happy to be back in contact with her. My mom told me I could stay with her. I did not process that thoroughly… I went through. And the look in Mo's eye's I knew I was making a bad decision. He didn't want me to go, but Mo again is a gentle spirit, never once controlling me.

I stayed with my mom for about a month in a half. Mo would come over and check on me. I felt safe and protected in his arms. I was so embarrassed of my life and I was confused as to why Mo still was around me. He had seen my ugly, my dad's ugly, and now my mom's ugly too. Mo also stuck around weeping eyes caused by the pain felt in the death of Steven. It was hard to cry in front of Mo about the death of another man; so, for the most part I suffered silently.

Another pain was when my mom stopped coming to the house where she and I were staying, I would wake up to the sound of nothingness. You would think the sound of nothingness would be peaceful, considering no crossfire of hate was surfacing. I listened for my mom's voice; but there was nothing. She left me in the house with some man that shared the same addition; he was just functional. I got the urge to call my aunt to see if I could stay with her again, she said no. As a result, I ended back with my dad; but before I left, I wrote my mom a letter in disgust. I was fed up with her lifestyle and how she continued to neglect me.

However, my feelings were hurt that my aunt didn't come to my rescue. I thought my aunt loved me and would do anything for me. My aunt had stability in her home and financials. Dragging out the remainder of high school was a heavy load. I hated school at this point. I wanted to run far away and not be reachable; but I voided my feelings and put smiles on others faces.

Between brokenness and lack of guidance, completing high school was goal, but I had no determination. I remember piercing my ears in the school's bathroom… that was a great way for me to release pain; it also drew me to the relation of my mom. Whenever my mommy came around, she made sure my ears were pierced and that I had earrings in. However, I had A's and B's and one incomplete. The class I never attended was the one I needed in order to meet the requirements for Core 40, but because I knew this class would actually require me to process and pay attention to details and know functions; I skipped it every day. Outside of meeting the requirements for graduation, I had to come up with money to pay for my cap and gown and additional fees needed.

I had no stability. I was forced to dig deeper in the emptiness that was the forerunner of my life. To redeem the strength to keep going was overwhelming. The level of sadness and having broken pockets cause me to have a nervous breakdown. Anxiety was the response to the chemical imbalances. I then began looking for help.

I reached out to another aunt. I asked if she could help me with my cap and gown. She agreed to help me if I repay her. At the time I agreed to repay her so that I could redeem the funds for graduation rather quickly. In the midst of that conversation, she learned of Steven's death and offered her assistance. This aunt was currently staying with the aunt who denied my arrival to her home prior going back to my dad's. However, somehow, I was able to move back in with my aunt based on negotiation.

In May of 2011, I graduated from Arsenal Tech High School. Excited? No, not really. I felt so embarrassed to walk across the stage. I asked myself, "Yanna, who are you really doing this for? Where is your wanted support system?" My parents were a no-show at my graduation. Sound familiar? I was sick to my stomach. I wanted them to be there. My heart filled with sadness as I met with my "supporters" after the ceremony. I was so excited to see my big cousin Ed. He was my favorite brother-cousin. However, I could hardly utter a word with warm heavy tears falling down my face. I tried to pretend to be happy. After greeting Ed, I looked for Mo in hopes that he had at least showed up… like that was his obligation. Crazy! It wasn't. I just loved him and wanted validation. Mo and I relationship ended May of 2011. I was detached from life. I could not run from all my disappointments fast enough.

Upon completion of high school, I had a goal in mind for college. I only wanted to go to college to get away from the constant reminder of neglect, embarrassment, and defeat. However, I didn't attend college right away. I had to repay my aunt first and figure out what I needed to do in order to go to college. I learned about Financial aid and applied. When it was time to place my parents' information; a ball appeared in my throat. All I could think of, "I know nothing about my parents that will help complete this form. I finessed the systems with numbers and information. The form was processed and now I had to wait.

During the waiting process, I had to find a job. Not only did I owe my aunt for the cap and gown, and other fees; I also had to begin looking for a job in order to have shelter. Every day I feared that I was going to be thrown out with nowhere to really go. However, before I landed a taxable job, I cleaned to repay senior fees. Once I met that goal, I was waiting to hear back from Amazon. Amazon was my first official job. I was getting paid 12.50 an hour, 40 hours a week. I felt like I was big balling. I had never had that much money coming in consistently. Working at Amazon taught me another stream of responsibility and how to conduct myself in a working environment.

I then had to pay my aunt's sister rent for housing me after she brought it to my attention that nothing was free in life. Aunty never gave me a set price, but every payday, I gave her 100. I was paid every week.

Outside of that, friction between the two sisters was created and my aunt no longer wanted to take me to work; in fact, she wanted us both to leave. I pleaded with my aunt to let me stay until I went to college. However, I was still waiting to see if I got approved for financial aid. I had to find my own way to work carrying burdens. My aunt's sister then started taking me to work after applying for the job herself. That didn't last long. She got put out. I was stressed out. My aunt then started taking me to working and picking me up. When it was close to my shift ending, I always worried if my ride was going to be out there. Some days I had to wait hours.

In January of 2012, I was awarded Financial Aid and was accepted to Vincennes University. The level of comfort swept over me. I now was faced with another dilemma. How was I going to get there? What do I need? I definitely figured it out and fast. I asked the head of the household: Aunty and her husband. She pointed me in the direction but did not provide any financial support. I had no money saved up because I was paying housing fees and buying my needs with wants. However, I did have money from my last check. I used every penny to get me to Vincennes, IN. I even had an overdraft fee. Never knew what that was until it hit my banking account showing - 100 something odd dollars. Thankfully, a check hit my school account after I registered for classes. I was careful with my spending because I knew I didn't have financial support.

Who R'U?
The who of being.

Dis'K

Have you ever heard a cracked CD play a track!
A deaf man read, or blind woman sign?
What about a bird with no wings???
But, has feet with feet with strings?
Play the track, I know it has cracks. Deaf man,
U heard love, that the blind woman could see.

January 3rd, 2012, I was enrolled in Vincennes University. I was on my own for the first time. I shed a few tears as I felt the emptiness in my dorm room. I was in an uncertain place. I was fearful that I would not be able to make it without the dysfunctional environments I was familiar with. I felt like I was jumping out of a plane with no survival tools. I was not prepared to be a student. In fact, I never cared to become one. I needed a place that provided stability. Learning material was something that came easy if I was interested.

As cycles of unlearned lessons from childhood reappeared during my beginning stages of womanhood; I found myself stuck in survival mode. I wanted to milk the system as much as I could because I saw what appeared to be overflow. My refund check was my best friend. My refund gave me access to resources that I never had. However, college made me pull from an empty bank.

I lacked knowledge on how to live a healthy lifestyle. As far as I could remember, the only deemed lessons were sitting around the dining room table listening to adult gossip; watching cups get empty out from liquor and burning cigarettes; with good food: witnessing abuse in various households that I shuffled through. Going to church faithfully, but never knowing how to connect with the Holy Spirit, but instead I was going through the emotions. Playing with dolls and toys was never me.

I couldn't wait to change my life, but I had no one at the time to point me in the direction on how to bring about effective change. I feared change because change always seemed to knock me ten steps backwards. I had freedom to walk, but I built a wall around me. I could not comprehend Truth. I was so stuck in the operation of generational curses that I failed to realize that I was keeping it going.

However, after about two weeks, Vincennes broke me in. Almost everyone knew who I was or at least what I looked like in flesh. I really didn't know how people knew me though, because I stayed to myself and only conversed with a few. I usually walked alone on the bricks; local bystanders tried to hustle me and reel me in, but I wasn't interested. I have always been particular about who I dated and respected. … and the only reason why I dated Wesley because I felt his struggle and he was gentle on the eyes and nose.

College was starting to feel like high school with student housing. However, in this immature setting, I felt independent for the first time in my life. My mind was trying to focus on a more mature matter; elevation, but my past had me caged. I often found myself trying to figure out how I ended up miles away from the burning nest. I questioned if I was capable of carrying the weight of change. I just wanted to be comfortable and dealt with correctly.

My roommate always welcomed me in the mix of her shenanigans. She got me again, only this time I didn't have to witness a fight. The roomie woke me up and asked me to come eat with her in TDC, our dining hall. I told her I would if she waited until I took a shower. Somehow, she managed to convince me that the shower would be there after we ate. I walked my little dirty butt to TDC and followed roomie to the table. Seated at the table ALREADY was roomie dude and some other dude I didn't know. Dude was cold too; it caught me off guard. I didn't pay too much attention to the setup that was already arranged between the three. I just knew I had a dirty butt and was ready to go back to my dorm. Nevertheless, I sat down at the table and learned the dude's name.

His lips were sealed in silence, yet his eyes were open when I looked at him. I said, "Umm He's cute and he smells good," speaking indirectly. Roomie laughed and then introduced us. She told me that he had been trying to figure out who I was. I instantly felt some type of way. In my head, I was thinking, "This chick a hater! Why would she let me come out knowing I'm not at my best, only to introduce me to this fine dude." I wanted to bash her head in the table. However, hope was not lost. He still was eager to figure out who I was.

Upon leaving TDC, I planned to head to the shower, but that was not the case. Instead, I walked aside the roomie to Morris Hall where the boys lived. We entered roomie's boyfriend room on a dead mission. Roomie and her dude were playing touchy feely, throwing candy around. Like always, roomie included me and tossed me the candy that her dude wanted! Boo didn't move a muscle, but instead observed my every move. It didn't take me long to get irritated. I told the roomie I was out. I was done playing 'Go Fish' with her.

I flew out of Morris Hall. Boo followed behind me. I knew he wanted to talk to me, but I was going to see if he was going to chase me. I began walking fast. Hey now, these little 2-foot legs can move now.

"Aye, yo Yanna!"

I kept walking.

Boo then put a little pep in his step.

I stopped and flashed him with a smile.

With excitement, I said, "YES!"

"Can I have your number?"

I answered, "NO, but I'll take yours.

February 7th, 2012 "we" made it "official."

I danced with my heart at the forefront. I had no idea how brainwashed I was. Love for me was nothing more than a pleasant feeling. If one could make me feel good, I loved em'. If you hurt me after I trusted you with the remaining pieces of my heart, my learned thuggish behavior and a pool of hidden demons would come to seek revenge.

I wanted to love unconditional; but my love was toxic and problematic. Boo didn't make it any easier. We stayed under each other 24/7 since day one. I felt incomplete whenever he left my side. I always wanted Boo around me to pass the hours of day. I hated when he departed from me, whether it was work-related or just him trying to enjoy his youth. My youth was destroyed and as a result, I was trying to control him. The fear of Boo not coming back when he left was sickening.

Boo could have had my life. I loved him so much that I would lay my life down so he could live. Crazy right?

Boo catching me in his arms when I'd run and jump, gave me a sense of protection. I felt unmovable in his arms. Seeing his eyes sparkle gave me light, hope. Boo made me feel like I had value, like I was important. I saw him as the King he is, I just gave him too much credit. I praised him instead of God. Boo became my god, unknowingly. Whatever he wanted, I yielded and paid attention to his needs and wants.

During Spring break of 2012, Boo and I rode down to Fort Wayne, IN, to celebrate Resurrection Sunday and for me to formally meet his parents. As we pulled into the driveway, I had no anxiety. I just couldn't wait to stretch my legs; after being crammed for about 5 hours in a little car with a few college students.

Once welcomed inside Senior's home, I noticed the structure and maturity of the environment. However, Senior respectfully accepted my presence and told me where I was to sleep through the night. I was right by his bedroom, in the guest room. The temperature in the house was very chill. I was freezing. I wanted my Boo!

The next stop was to greet Boo's mom. Her big smile and open arms greeted me as the door opened. Within minutes of our arrival, she asked me endless questions. She voiced that Boo, and I were not to be making any children any time soon. Little did she, or even I know, in my womb was a child, preparing to take its first breath soon. At the time, I didn't know I was with child, but I guess I should have known. Boo and I planned our Firstborn. He wanted to impregnate me, and I was all for it for selfish reasoning's. However, the meet-and-greet- with Boo's parents was successful. I believed I passed the first test…. Nobody warned me that there would be more to come.

Sunday morning, we attended worship service at The Destiny Dome Embassy @ Cathedral of Praise International located in Fort Wayne, Indiana. Going to church was a normal routine for me. I've been in church since the time I could remember. I've given my life to Christ, by confession with my mouth that Jesus was Lord. I was baptized in the name of: The Father, Son, and Holy Spirit: Trinity. Now the other part is, I didn't truly believe in my heart that Jesus died for me. However, there was something different about this particular church; just didn't know what it was. Years later, I fully understand the connection and still till this day, I am forever grateful to be part of this dynamic Grace ministry.

Boo and I returned to VU to our normal routine. I had no worries as long as I had Boo with me. Boo and I broke the laws daily to make sure we accommodated each other. We had that 'I'll pull you through the window after-hours' type of situation; a risk-it-all relationship, with no remorse for breaking the rules. Though Boo was always present with me, I told him to prove his love for me; as a result, he tattooed my name on the right side of his rib.

I loved Boo. He was different! He stood out amongst them all, so he definitely was up for grabs when we met. I instantly connected with him. He towered over me; he could pick me if he had good balance. Boo appeared to be headstrong, self-motivated, and determined. I felt like he could take the lead in my life. Whatever he lacked I encouraged him through letters and placed them in his notebooks or book bag. What's crazy is my heart let me feel the need and pain of others; meanwhile my heart was broken, in shambles. I never dealt with heart breaks. I just grew numb to them all. However, I just knew Boo was for me. It was like God had set him aside just for me. Could it be?

Before leaving school for summer break, Boo and I decided to get a pregnancy test. The pregnancy was confirmed instantly. We were excited, but the excitement soon vanished when reality hit. Boo and I had to split and go separate ways: Indianapolis, IN for me Fort Wayne, IN for him. We also had to find a way to tell our parents; but as for me I had no parents that cared. I was headed back to my secondary home, surprisingly. I feared that I wouldn't make it the full summer living with aunty; especially after telling her I was with child.

Speak

Why won't silent lips speak?
Are you weak?
Are you embarrassed? Ashamed?!
You knew better or did you know?
Are you still untamed?
Don't hide,
Come on,
Gather your thoughts for your baby's name.

As blood filled the rim of the toilet, I was having a panic attack. Immediately I thought I'd lost my baby. I stayed in the bathroom to gather my thoughts. I had to tell my aunt that I was pregnant. I was so nervous. I guess I stayed in the bathroom a little too long; aunty called my name and asked if I was okay. I gave her hesitant 'no.'

Concerned, she responded,

"What's wrong?"

I nervously answered,

"I don't know. I see a lot of blood."

"Well are you on your period?"

"No!" I replied quickly.

"Well, are you pregnant, Yanna?"

My thoughts were getting the best of me rooting in anxiety. I was anxious to know the outcome once the truth had proof. I was silent for a good ten seconds. Those seconds felt like ten hours. I finally answered in fear, "No! I don't think so." The lies... I tell you. I knew from the moment I peed on the stick back at VU; before I touched foot back into her home that I was pregnant. The only honest truth was, I didn't know how many weeks.

Later that day aunty took me to hospital and learned I was pregnant. It took me by surprise that my aunty wasn't angry with me and told me to get out. She actually was happier than I was, but that soon changed when my uncle came home and learned about the conception. My uncle told me how disappointed he was in me. The disappointment showed a level of care. However, when aunty saw that he was upset, her reaction was distasteful.

Watching aunty switch like a light made me distance myself. I didn't trust her to bring me comfort. All the questions that I wanted to ask her went right out the window. I no longer desired for her to be a part of the baby talk. I just wanted to remain with shelter and have a level of security for my insanity. However, I feared that if I voiced my concerns, auntie's generosity would run dry and evict me out of her home. I then realized I was in a sinking ship. Afraid I was.

.... I for a long time adored my aunt in my adolescence years because she appeared to be everything I wanted out of life. She had the resources that Winthrop lacked. I would replay her wedding video over and over. I loved seeing my sister, and I throwing flowers down the ale; and hearing the song: Up Where We Belong by Bebe and CeCe Winans.

Aunty took care of me after her mother passed, my grandmother. She did my hair for the holidays. Brought me clothes to match her fly. She taught me how to budget and be responsible with my money. I even went to church with her faithfully every Sunday. However, she never taught me or how to honor correctly. She would tell me to stay in a kid's place. But how? I was never a kid. I didn't have time to enjoy my youth. My youth was robbed from me. I was more concerned with the why's in life.

.... Aunty played a major role in trying to fulfill a mothering role in my life; but I still felt a huge voidance.

The memories of crying for my mom long nights after hearing her voice replay, but never seeing her was mental abuse. I reflect visiting my mom in work release; or strung out on the streets. The memories of my mom are not the healthiest. I remember my mom taking money from my sister and having us walk with her to trap houses. However, my mom had a troubled youth. She had deep rooted pains that she never dealt with that caused her to abandon all five of her children and herself. No matter what though, whenever I was in the presence of my mom, I showed value to her being. I would dress her up, put lip gloss on her, give her my clothes that she could fit, and feed her. I loved my mom no matter what. I wanted to help her the best way possible, I just didn't know how.

So, I said that to say; I longed for a mother's love. A mother that would teach me about men and how to be a lady.... to pour into me so that I'll be ready when the knuckleheads came with pressure that I liked. I wanted a mother that taught me how to be a meek spirit and prepare me to be a wholesome woman and wife. A mother that would nurse me back to life.

I looked outside of myself to fill the years of discomfort when the whole time I should have been looking inside myself. I never knew.

However, I learned from the various women around me. First being my grandmother. She became ill with cancer and left me in 2002. I felt like rotten milk. The other women I watched were my aunts, cousins, babysitters, and friends. I started to pursue their qualities that they displayed openly. I watched homes get built from the ground up. I watched broken intellect graduate college. I watched delicious meals being prepared and served. I watched hair being dressed; and later watched one of the various women own her own shop and collect booth rent. I watched bills getting laid out and paid. I watched dogs get more love than human life. I also watched broken spirits be unhappy: gossiping and blaming others for their frustrations. I watched hate fester when others completed a task first. I watched dust get overlooked and deemed as lived clean. I watched abusers play victims. I watched support root from a self-centered place. I watched caring become a burden. Selfishness. I watched hoopdies get upgraded to designer brands. I watched laughter last less than pain. I watched working hands never stop, even when they were tired and didn't feel like working. More importantly I watched wives not have a meek spirit, and discredit the man of the household, taking control. I watched

Sunday's best get dressed and look the part; but never being fully engaged and transforming the outcome of their lives.

These unhealthy learned dysfunctions made a healthy relationship; almost impossible. Though I could cook, clean, organize, budget, and was educated; the negative pulled more weight. I was forced to think about marriage when I lack the proper resources. I didn't know what a wife was. To my understanding a wife wasn't nothing more than a woman that could cook, clean, have a job, be a little smart, and know how to please her man. As pressure continued for marriage; I talked myself into being ready. I knew I met the underlining standards of a wife; however, being a wife, as I learned, requires way more than just those underlying standards.

However, I started pressuring marriage on Boo. If Boo and I weren't talking about marriage, the visitation rights were slim to none. There was a certain time that Boo could only come see me. I was told after nine, he had to go. I understood that, but what I had a hard time understanding was how he was going to do that when he lived in Fort Wayne and worked every day passed the hour. There was no way he could get off work, drive to Indianapolis, and be gone by nine. That was a waste of time and a thought. Boo was able to visit once, post baby.

Back to the marriage thing. Though marriage was desirable for me then, I didn't know what a wife REALLY was. I didn't have oneness with myself; let alone trying to bind and yoke with a man I barely knew. He was fine, smart, etc… I knew he knew God and had a supportive family. Dassit. Marriage was not desirable for Boo. He wasn't hearing the marriage ideas that I was bombarding him with; it actually started pissing him off.

However, whenever I pitched a play for me to visit Boo, I hit a strike. I finally struck out. There was no way I was going to ignore the fact that my child's father was in another city trying his hardest to make his way to me. I, of course, felt I needed his presence. I made my mind up to undermine authority. I left and drove to Fort Wayne with Boo. I was given an ultimatum; that if I left to go to Fort Wayne for the weekend, I could not come back to what home was considered to be. I never told Boo what authority said, I just told him come on. Boo pulled up. My possessions were snatched out of my hands and dumped out... "That's my damn bag!" and slammed the door shut. I politely gathered my things and headed to Fort Wayne.

Nevertheless, I came back to pure destruction. The promise was kept. I wasn't able to step foot back in my secondary home. My things were packed in black trash bags. I was now homeless with a baby in my stomach. My disobedience caused this chain reaction. If I never left to visit my child's father, I would have still had shelter. Being a misled youth, made it hard to decipher whether I was being protected or controlled.

In July of 2012, I lived with Susan B. for the remainder of the summer. Susan has been around me since I was 8 years old. I met her through my dad. She also played in the band at our church, Olivet Missionary Church Baptist Church. I gave my life to Christ at Light of the World Christian Church, with my grandmother; I was baptized at OMBC; A personal decision. However, Susan was one of the ones I could trust! I felt comfortable with her. Never once has she approached me like she was my mother or authority figure, she treated me like a friend. Susan was in fact my best friend. We spent most of the days in laughter. It was as if God whispered in her ear about me. Susan was very careful with my heart; somehow, in my brokenness, I was repairing hers.

During the summer while living with Susan, a former colleague, La, passed away. Her death felt beyond weird. One minute, I was braiding her hair in my dorm room, and the next, I'm overseeing her body laid in the stillness of a coffin. La's death was heartbreaking. She tried her hardest to change her ways. She was even introduced to Oprah; I too someday in the near have hopes to speak with Oprah. My grandmother stayed watching "The Color Purple." However, La was a great athlete and friend.

After La's funeral, I returned to a state of confusion. The emptiness I was experiencing caused me to grieve more. I started seeing vivid pictures of loved one's caskets flash before me, memorials in some cases. I grieved silently, becoming a silent sufferer. I used the pains of my former, for a reason to cry in that current season. I needed a reason to cry so I could release the frustrations, rage, and anger that was deeply embedded within.

I was all over the place with my emotions. I'm laughing in public and crying in the pillows that attest. My heart was aching in pain. The pain moved from death; to birthing life. My pregnancy had been approved and welcomed by my boyfriend; to now hearing that I needed to get a DNA test. I was extremely confused and didn't know where this angle was coming from. I then questioned Boo and started doubting his love for me. I then reminded him that he knew this was his baby... we planned it. However, the doubt was coming from an authoritative role; which started causing division between me and Boo. I started hating him; but still desired him.

I felt dark in spirit, disconnected from light. If I weren't pregnant, I would have thought that I was just existing to collect waste. Boo drove to Indy and spent the night with me over Susan's; though I was hurt, I silenced my ill will in his presence and tried to love him unconditionally. I knew that he knew, the baby was his; just didn't understand why he was defending me. It was like he was scared or something… I hated it; and again started to remove love. I was no longer in love with Boo and my actions started seeping through. However, I did still want to love him.

After a long drought with no parental communication, I contacted my pops to see if he could finally assist with my needs. Pops was able to be a responsible parent and complete the task of driving me back to school. I felt like he owed me a drive back to college, since he missed almost all of my accomplishments thus far. Nevertheless, I packed up for college and headed to Winthrop.

Before returning to Vincennes, I had a doctor's appointment to determine the sex of the baby; boo met me in Indianapolis. Boo and I found out were having a BOY. When I got to Winthrop, I was happy to discuss the news with my pops.

"Daddy! Daddy!"

"What?!!!" he screamed.

"Daddy, I'm having a baby boy," I said softly.

I really wanted to burst out in tears because pops drew me to an instant image of my childhood: the harsh and uncaring tone of his voice, the obvious distaste to continue the conversation… I quickly left before he could see a teardrop. I went upstairs with Boo. I was so embarrassed, more embarrassed than the filth that covered every level of the house. Boo and I were literally in the middle of the mice den. Boo laid with me on a stale, dirty mattress that my dad borrowed from the alley…. I'm not certain actually about this mattress; but yes, shopping in people's trash was deemed the norm. However, the whole Winthrop operating system was broken.

Later that day, before pops took me back to school, my mom appeared: seemed to be out of nowhere. I remember her eating like she was missing meals regularly. I was distraught. I just looked at my mother as if she was an unfamiliar face. I was praying that Boo stayed upstairs with the mice, so he wouldn't see my mom. I didn't want Boo to witness her off her high. I felt caged in. I fought to keep my eyes open so I wouldn't cry.

'Momma!'

She looked up. I didn't say another word. I just stood in the doorway and looked her over. She looked so lifeless; it disturbed my peace. Sadness filled my body. I hadn't seen my mom in a year and some change. The last I saw her was for a day, back before she left me in the house with a functioning addict. What a way to start off my second semester of college. I left sight of my mother so I could find my pops.

"Dad. Are you ready to go? I don't want to be late signing in." Pops must have thought I cursed his name. He cussed me out so bad, my ears left. My eyes grew big with embarrassment. I was hoping Boo didn't hear him cursing me out. I sent Boo on his way and told him I'd meet him at school. In the meantime, my question was left unanswered. Another hour passed, and I was terrified to ask if pops was ready again, but he yelled, "READY!" Pops ushered my mom out the door. In her hands, she held a variety of undesirable foods.

.... I made it back to Vincennes, fall of 2012. I was about 5 months pregnant with D3 upon my return to my dorm in Vigo Hall.

Fall

I'm falling,
But no one is there to catch me.
I'm falling.
My knees are weak.
Like, autumn beating leaves in trees.

During my second semester at Vincennes, Boo started noticing how damaged I really was. I was carrying the burdens of yesterday into the newness of day. My hormones and other chemical imbalances crossed paths as weeks passed. I had so much running through my mind; I couldn't escape it all. I started becoming abusive to Boo because that's all I knew. I just wanted to fight. I started to see the love of my life as a target.

I watched my dad beat people into control. If he didn't want them to leave, say a word, or stay; he would beat them. Not only did I physically abuse Boo, I used verbal abuse; another learned dysfunction that I learned from various households.

Whenever I didn't get my way; there was abuse to the tenth power. How sickening is this learned behavior; just sick! Boo did nothing wrong; but want to enjoy life. Not only did my insecurities try to stand in the way, but my despaired thought pattern was also chopped and crewed.

No matter what, Boo took in the abuse and never once put his hands on me. He actually gave more love; until I started embarrassing him… then he became rough with me and I did not like it! I loved him and just didn't know how to show it correctly. I remember standing out on the bricks screaming pay for an abortion since you want to put your friends before me with my robe on. …Knowing good and well, an abortion was never an option.

Still, Boo returned to my dorm room and held me through the night. He also drove to every doctor's appointment; no questions asked. He held and rubbed my belly. He also talked to our prince everyday while he was growing and developing.

Never once did my ungrateful butt say thank you. Whew! I felt like I deserved every good treatment given. Thank you's were at a distance. I showed my appreciation in other ways; like sex and buying little stuff like socks and t-shirts… food. Boo and I ate out every day like we were already rich.

However, the semester was ending, and winter break was approaching. I was due to give birth to my prince, January 4th of 2013. In the in-between time, I reconnected with my aunt. Aunty allowed me to come stay with her yet again. Aunty and Unk made sure I went to my remaining doctor's appointments and made as comfortable as possible this go round. They even went as far as making space for my son to have his own room. Aunty bought most of my baby's needs. I have to say my son had everything he needed post-birth, except for a healthy mom.

Despite my ugly ways and thoughts, I received help. I bashed my aunt for months in my head and gossiped about her as well. I hated how our relationship grew to be after my adolescent years. I ended looking foolish because the very person I bashed, was willing to provide for me.

Condolence

Did you put the "E" in Help Me?

Then, why are my thoughts of you so ugly.

Is it: Empathy or Sympathy?

Did you understand or pity me?

It wasn't your fault: My life I was delt was a misfortune.

I needed comfort and support; but it was all gone too soon.

I admit; I blame you. I then hated you; then Jesus reminded me that his words were still true. I then saw encouragement that's been you. I believe this is my condolence to you. I know I bruised you too. I am sorry and together we can get through. I just thought you were going to be my Momma and that failed through. We made in this year; to the new... So let start to finish with I LOVE YOU.

Seve'N

Three!
You! Not me, nor we!
D3
Tweet signs noted with life's melodies.
Me; no, we,
Crossing t's in defeat.
You; no, me,
Couldn't see through the eyes of the enemy.
Seven is complete.
We rushed and kept adding three plus three.
Grace added seven times three.

On January 2nd, 2013, a prince was born. My son's birth sent light to a dark place in my life. I felt like I had something to live for. I wanted to be the mother I never had. I could not wait to hold my baby and love on him in the best way possible. When I held D3, I never counted his toes. I knew he was whole. I was drawn to my baby's eyes. His eyes reflected God's face. He also had a pleasant smell of newness that I wanted to preserve.

Upon leaving Community North Hospital, my next destination was home. It was a long, bumpy car ride to my domains. I was extremely sore while recovering surgery. Ms. Naomi nurtured me until it was time for her to return to work.

After Naomi left, I was due for my baby's first doctor's visit. I vividly remember aunty driving me to my appointment in a cold truck. Aunty heat went out in her truck; it wasn't a harsh punishment… though it felt like it. Aunty made me carry the car seat with the base. She knew I wasn't in the best condition to be carrying all that; I had a C-section. I thought to myself… "This is payback for the ill thoughts I had toward her over the summer and into fall."

However, moving forward, Aunty and Unk covered the rest of my needs. They were already doing more than enough by letting me be there rent-free. I didn't have any money, just baggage and a live bill. The strength from Unk's working hands released tension in my stomach muscles as he wrapped my stomach tightly. Food was brought to me so I wouldn't have to walk to the kitchen. Aunty informed me the best ways to maneuver throughout the house without straining my muscles. They also held and cared for D3, releasing me to the comfort of fresh sheets.

I needed help, and for two weeks straight, all I was receiving was help. Strangely enough, all help isn't good help. I didn't realize that the birthing of my son was opening pains in my beloved aunt. As I reflect, D3 was shaping Robert. I began feeling like I had no control over the seed I carried to life with the help of God. I felt like my aunt was trying to take the very thing I birth. She didn't just want to help me; she wanted to control my motherhood. I then considered my housing being a hidden agenda, so that a baby could be present. These are only my thoughts and feelings... Right?!

I grew depressed. I felt for my aunt as I kept feeling her birthing pains out of the result of the stillness in her wounding. However, it was out of my reach to fill her void. I had my own problems and worries; I didn't have the answers to hers. My living condition became toxic for my mind. I was trying to reason within myself.

"Aunty isn't trying to control me. She doesn't have a hidden agenda... She's simply trying to help, stop with the mind games Yanna. She's there to help you, not hurt you. Help and not hurt... What about love? Does she love me? What is love? Love is love right... Ugh. Why do I feel like I'm on eggshells then? Is that love? Is that support? You don't have nothing Yanna! No job. No other support. Stop tripping. Tripping gone have you homeless if she can even smell it. Now Unk, may be able to save you if your mind exposes you; maybe, even if she doesn't want him to. If you are feeling this bad leave, what's holding you? Fear Hello! I'm scared. I can't just leave. My womb is still healing. Plus, my son!!!!!!!!!!!!!!!!!!!!!!!!!!!!!! My Baby!!!!!!!!!!!!! He needs security more than me. He can't defend for himself... well you can't defend for yourself, right?!........ Ugh my mind, get out of my head!"

The toxicity! I had so much pressure on me I didn't know where to turn nor what voices to listen to.

After voicing my needs for more diapers for the appropriate size, I was told that if any help was going to continue that I needed to place Boo on child support! "Child support; a broken woman's sport?" I thought to myself. Man, there was no way I was doing that. My son was only two weeks old with an active father. Boo was also in college at Defiance. Boo had no problem driving to see us and providing what we needed. So, child support! Really. NO ma'am. However, I just reasoned with her, and agreed to place Boo or child support; just to silence the noise. In the meantime, I was thinking of a way to escape because support was ending if I didn't place Boo on child support. In my mind that meant I'd soon be without shelter. I was thrown out numerous times before; I knew it was nothing for it to done again.

Silenced anger and rage formed. For the last time, I knew I had to leave and not return seeking shelter. I was tired of being controlled and forced into a world I did not belong. I heard clearly; even with my own voice clouding my head. I made a major move while she and Unk were away from the house. I called Boo to inform him about the child support verbiage. He wasn't having it. Remember now we are 18: both Boo and I (1993). Boo sent his mother to come get his family.

My two-week-old son and I left aunties' home unexpectedly and unannounced; it truly was a move of dishonor. However, I get a pass because I was never taught the right way. I believed leaving the way I did would diffuse verbal, physical, and mental abuse. The street taught me that if you don't like something, do something about it with no explanation. I also felt safe in the hands of Naomi. I believed that she would give the proper care to me and her grandson.

Skipped

Mommy, why you run?
That's a handicap undone.
Now you can't crawl but stand as One.
Shackled bars,
Blocking defeat, that was sought as won.
We don't get redoes but renews to unite.
The ones,
Whose oppression came back and stung.
See, you thought victory was won,
But your fight has just begun.

As we touched down in Fort Wayne, I embraced the smell of fresh flowers. I felt like a lily in the valley. Living arrangements that were suitable for my son and I. Beds were turned over for our comfort. Exceeding my known needs were being met, not knowing the depths I have gone to be free. Undeserving grace paved the way for my feet to be. I went to church faithfully with my seed.

On Sunday, February 3rd, 2013, Apostle Dr. Oscar J. Nelson Dowdell-Underwood, Jr., PhD, blessed my son and gave him back to the Lord at The Destiny Dome Embassy @Cathedral of Praise Int. Fort Wayne, Indiana. At that moment, I didn't know how much protection came with releasing my baby back to Glory. I went to church with the same learned religious point of view that was passed down to me years prior. So, going to church was a normal routine. I went through the motions, took good notes; but never applied them to my life. I loved how encouraging the words were, but I didn't know how to Trust the Word of God. The core of my brokenness was getting covered with layers of emotional feel-goods. At night, I went back and laid down with familiar demons, sometimes new ones. In my darkest moments, my son bought a sense of peace and healing as I watched him grow. He brought togetherness and real, genuine love and affection to his surrounding family. No matter the hardships I was suffering from, holding my son made me come back to a place of love. Oddly enough, I knew real love had finally begun. However, I grew afraid because nothing good was ever consistent in my life, except Grace. I feared that I would fail my baby. My insides began to cry as I knew it wasn't me fully taking care of him. The very thing I ran from with aunty caught up with me; the only difference I now had a job. I worked at Kroger's doing night stock. I didn't have the tools to fight; I just clung to Boo whenever he was in sight. Boo was attending college down the road at Defiance College. I looked forward to his regular weekend visits.

One thing about Boo, I'd go to war for him. I didn't want anyone else hurting him nor causing him any pain. Granted I caused some discomfort, but I'm me... make sense, no not really: I get that too.... I never wanted to hurt Boo. That was never my intent. EVER; and when he hurt my feelings... I'd speak on it raising conflict. I was at awe. Boo seemed to have a picture-perfect life. Both of his parents were functional and educated, whereas mines were completely opposite. My stomach turned sour when I begin to see boo hurting. My mind took me there. I begin to wonder if Boo wasn't top priority, then what was his family? Seeing someone trying to purposely destroy the core of peace in one's being made me go into defensive mode.

It was extreme to watch the pain move throughout Boo's body starting with his eyes. I felt it was my right and responsibility defend him. I wanted him to know, no matter what, he had top priority in the lives of his family. I wanted to snatch back the words of hate. After hate was spoken, the atmosphere shifted, and disrespect was present. I no longer felt loved and protected.

Senior's home was like a Presidential Suite. There was a vibe that echoed throughout the house. One could tell what kind of man Senior was when they stepped foot in his home. Every room was dressed accordingly. He looked like money, smelled like money, and had money. Businessman across the board with a level of leadership that I've never seen before in a man.

I will admit it was hard living with Senior, only because he oversaw everything in his household; as he should. However,

I was very private, and I felt like I didn't need his parental guidance. Plus, there was a level of guilt present. I felt like a was a burden on this family. I felt I like I no longer belong, because I felt poor; whereas my surroundings were rich. I didn't want to answer any questions about my life and where I was going. Why? because I did not know where my life was headed myself. I was just out on a lim. I was 19 with no family support and lacked guidance.

I was present in his home a few months later; and had no choice but to respect him… Which was hard; because the depth of the pain, frustration, and hurt between me and his son for not standing with me…when I would indeed go to war for him no matter what.

However, mediocrity wasn't tolerated around Senior. He showed tough love; and absolutely nothing was going to come between him and his son. The level of protection Senior had around his boy was unbelievable. It was actually tight; but scary. I had never seen a father love his son in that manner; never. Whatever Senior said, Boo did; or tried to meet expectations. Boo wanted to be his dad in fact. Which, in many ways Senior was a great role model. Again, he had resources that most lacked.

Gre'y

When the leaves withered away,
My pain stayed.
I hid in the branches,
Hoping I wouldn't crack and break away.
Fragile, I was.
Thinking the pain would just vanish,
leave the tree,
But it rained,
And the pain stayed and multiplied by three.
I reached out, but nothing was around me!
I had joy in the things my night eye I could see.
Beyond my reach,
The moon lit the night skies,
And the stars sparkled like loud cries.
As seasons changed,
my hurt remained.
I was unsure what to do,
I smoked trees that "high" knew.
I knew,
That GREY skies are not blue!

Upon leaving Senior's house, Boo taught me how to drive and I received my license. I enrolled in school at Indiana State University, and Boo followed the pursuit.

In August of 2013, Boo, myself, and our son was established in Terre Haute, IN. I had my son on my hip. From the moment I stepped in Terre Haute, I hated it. I was already doubtful about moving again. There was no peace within the family. I was trying to adapt to a new living environment, but I just couldn't get past the grey areas. Shortly after moving into our apartment together, Boo Split and parted ways. I began smoking weed heavy to numb the pain. I fell into depression. I would cry and stare at myself in the mirror. I investigated the mirror as if it was going to give me answers. I was searching for my identity. I didn't understand my purpose in life, other than being a great mom. My confidence was shot. I was unhappy with myself. I didn't love me. I hate the skin I was in. I wanted Boo to bring me happiness.

I lost about 34 pounds. I felt like life sucked me up and left me to die. I was facing postpartum depression and had no idea. I was stressed out. I knew I had to still take care of my son no matter what I felt like. I had no one to teach me how to be a mother; but my son, himself. That little handsome boy gave me the endurance I needed to keep going. Lowering my son's awareness of our broken home was goal. I took my son to the park, prayed with him, taught him, and of course cooked him healthy balanced meals. I loved my son more than I loved myself. For that reason, I protected him the best way possible. I never bashed Boo because I still loved him. When he called, I answered. When he came over, he had access to the inside. I treated him no different.

I shielded my pains from my son, and for the most part it was effective. Soon as I put my baby to sleep; it was time to roll a fatty. Actually, I didn't know how to roll the blunts; I had the drug dealers do it until I learned. I soon started getting free weed. None of them would charge me, and the ones that tried … I'll say I'm coo I'll have my other guy come through. Petty. I knew how to get what I want without giving up the booty or performing any act. The only man my son knew was his dad. I wanted to protect that image, so he would always respect him.

It's crazy how I walked around looking flawless; meanwhile, I was a train wreck. Fine dudes offered to take me out and do this and that; I wasn't going. All I was thinking about was getting back to my son and doing our normal routine; and when Boo called that was the other true male connection. Hearing Boo's voice made me sad all over again. I wanted to be where he was; but he was enjoying life without me. I stayed at Indiana State another year. By this time, I had moved three times. I hated moving; I related it as a sign of inconsistency and failure.

In the summer of 2015, I found an apartment while visiting Boo. In July of 2015, I moved into Country Club apartments on the Southside of Indianapolis, due to a high level of forced guilt. Within a couple weeks, Boo joined me. We were back SHAKING. I was far removed from God. I was immoral. Pouring from an empty bank. Just smoking trees that high knew…... and enjoying putting laughter in the hearts of others…. That kept me smiling.

When You Smile

My world is alright when you smile.

Just smile,

Your smile it glosses,

Pulling my love through for you.

I don't wanna see you down;

Just smile.

My world is alright when you smile.

Your smile,

Gives me reason to press, and stick around.

Just Smile.

It brings, joy and peace…

I began to feel like love is working me.

Just Smile.

My world is alright when you smile.

Pla'y

"Have a seat in the ground,"
"No!"
"Why not now? You've been playing in the devil's playground."
"So! I rather have a seat on the Merry-Go-Round, where a birthing of Jesus, with no DNA of man is found. Mary birth Jesus to be: That of Grace, Favor, and Mercy; You know, True Love to Peace." "Get off my ride' I'll still find a crack, I'm the devil… I still want you on my slide.'"Look, Jesus died for me… I know I gave you my soul. It wasn't intentional! Know that deep waters come to and fro; but it was the living water there Profound! Giving life to death for those who hear and are found. I have peace knowing, I have dominion over the birds chirping in the devil's playgrounds; pretending to be joyous sounds. Look even falling leaves, keep color and take a bow, acknowledging, that new seasons of life is showering down."
"Just sit down!" "Ugh… ok."
"Lay down"
"Play…
… oh I see you; you think you got me down.
You know my weakness and what keeps my bound.
You uncircumcised philistine, I don't belong to you! Cut me loose. I'm not scared of you. A virgin birth Jesus for me. Confused? I must Allow Truth to be One, like the Birthing Mary found. Mary-Go-Round. Not the devil's playground."

The things you run from are still attached to you! You MUST face your fears! YOUR FEARS CANNOT OVERTAKE YOU, UNLESS U ALLOW UR FAILURES TO. I was fearful; to write… but I wrote; and will continue…write. I was fearful to go after my destiny… but here we are. There's a Dream, Alive in you. When you're able to look failure in the eye and not cry…. When you're able to release that slavery mentality; you're then able to see to believe. We cannot walk around blaming folk; rather they hurt us are not. It's Jesus, ready to carry you and fight. Learning to not conform to this world; is hard, yes; but the Word tells us not to for a reason. The world isn't meant for Believers to conform to it; but stand victorious in it; for the Earth is temporary. If we pass the test on Earth, surely God has prepared us a place in Heaven after this life.

Now the test in life; shouldn't embarrass you; for the greatest of great have failed in the Earth. Jesus, himself was temped and had to pray for strength. Which leads me to say… prayer works when you believe. You don't have to be all fancy with your words. Just believe. Jesus felt your prayer and heard you clearly. Often, we think God didn't hear us… wrong! He did, our prayers may be very well working against the plans for our life. However, God will grant us the desires of our heart for His Glory.

So, when you're getting beat up living in this life… Remember your prayers… Remember your thoughts. Remember your word. The devil is busy; just like God. So a stubborn vessel; the devil dwells there... until an authorized

79

power decrees and declare that demon be released in Jesus' name.

During, 2015 - 2017, I completely lost myself in idolatry. I was shaking and voiding the precepts of God. Convenience and comfort were the root of my evil. From Wesley to Moe and Boo, I caught five more bodies... totaling eight. I was told a cat gets only nine lives." .... I had to stop before mine died. GRACE.

I was ushered into this sinful life; by the very woman I trusted. Though I was ushered; the choice was mine. I didn't want to hurt any more, but I didn't know how to stop the pain. I cut my hair, in hopes to alter my identity. I started going back to church, but I'd smoke a blunt before entering, so I could be numb. I also began going to Bible Study. Pastor Moore was speaking true conviction and I was attracted to the knowledge I was receiving. However, I didn't know how to stop being immoral; nor did I want to take on the responsibility of my adult life; it was painful for me to be removed from my comfort state. I was stuck in the past of 1995; only to continue to grow and experience levels of abuse that shaped a fearful life I dreaded.

... (i) wanted my dad to be: A protector. Loving and Caring. A teacher. A man with big dreams, goals, and ambition; nothing obscure. A strong leading man was desired. One that paid attention to my needs and wants; and did not argue but take charge without being controlling. One that didn't beat women or disrespect their temples.

Having a man in my presence that was checking off my list. I was naive, relaxed, and too comfortable. Men became gods to me and the only One true living God allowed me to endure great pain. The pain was so unbearable; as a result, I chose to converse with another broken spirit more than Jesus Christ. Aunty appeared to be a whole, gentle, stable, and vibrant, elegant woman.

I was venting to the very woman that had access to the world influenced by hell's gates. What attracted me to her was acknowledging the fact she had cancer like her mom, my grandmother, and her outer elegance and her love language. However, I wanted her to be as comfortable as possible while she was going through her treatments; meanwhile, I got too comfortable. I trusted her judgment; and while I was helping her, I began to feel like I needed her. Her laughter mixed with mine felt like healing to the soul. Long nights out; healthy five-star dates, and fresh mani's and pedi's were fun times. After all, I longed for a mother. My aunt seemed to be a perfect fit. She seemed so peaceful. Her outer beauty and the way she appeared to the eye and nose; I thought she was A1. What I sought peace for, was an idol stillness. I wanted my emotions to be silenced. I wanted peace to experience true happiness and wealth: those were a couple things that aunty focused on outside of men. She also wanted to just wake up a millionaire, away from the drama that filled our everyday lives.

My darkened spirit was pulled and submerged with auntie's. Whenever I was with my aunt, she would massage me after long talks about how to get over the man that I truly desired every day. Soon liquor was in the mix. One occasion a pill became part of the mix.... knowing I didn't do either, it worked its way into managing my broken heart. Talks about how sex with new partners will make me lose sight of Boo drew a conclusion to do so.

After spending days, weeks, and months with aunty, I started noticing that the Buddha dolls were not just decorations; and the affirmation of inner peace and reincarnation came from an altered mind. Every time I felt sick or just wanted to be in a relaxed state; liquor and a pill was offered. I remember telling aunty, "No! I remember that half of a pill made me sicker than I felt before I took it. I smoke weed dassit." Do you have some weed?" "NO; but we can go get some."

I remember the whole room was spinning and I was nauseated but couldn't throw up. Aunty then rubbed lotus, a crystal rock she named on the painful spots of my body; everywhere but my heart and massage me until I drifted off in a deep sleep. Aunty then started making me part of her project practicing Reiki healing on me.

I remember an odd few coming over her house going in the back room doing chants. I asked aunty about her friends and their practices. She then told me they performed Reiki on her once before; and somehow, I associated Reiki with auntie's present condition: CANCER; but I didn't look too much into it.

After noticing that my aunt was involved in the Buddhist faith; I wanted to know more. I saw my aunt as intelligent and pure... again very peaceful and elegant. 'If practicing inner peace was good for aunty, sure enough it was good for me."

The Buddhist faith was crippling my beliefs in God. I was already mad at God because I just knew he failed me and didn't love me... because after all my life had been hell since I was in my mother's womb: to her not being able to withstand abuse and neglect in her former to present life. I was left at two; with no mother to hold on to.

Though I've always felt pure at heart for others, my heart led my soul astray. I was filled with loneliness. I was foolish in my processing. Instead of going to Jesus, I felt like I could handle myself on my own. I lit candles and listened to loved songs, while my waterfall was releasing water. I cleaned and made sure everything was in place. I went out in the city doing good deeds.... However, I was still disconnected from Jesus. Still disturbed by my mental; focusing on what I didn't have and what I wanted. There was disturbed peace in my home. The scent of a man made me feel like one was there; so, began pulling back on sex and trying to figure out who I was. I became depressed the more I thought about lack that's been my life. I wanted my mommy; but still strung out on crack.

Mommy to Me

My breath to life;
My soul, I won't let die;
without having peace and closure tied.
Mommy to me;
You're my true love with innocent feet.
My lavender, violet jewel.
Your smile: I have.
You're my beauty in my flower: Rose Gold.
Really Lily: I like that! Soft and pretty.
You're my sunflower; Spring, in May showers.
Mommy to me; forever holding hands…
Relating heart beats;
Healing rhymes, singing our favorite song.
Mommy to me, my shoulder; I see you getting strong.
Don't fold. Hold on a little longer.
Mommy to me;
You're my favorite love song laying in the rain with no clothes
on; Free… just enjoying the rain purifying soil strong.
Mommy to me; It's Ayanna Lea from you to me.

What's Love

Because you love me; premature death left me. Love gave addiction a ceased end. It was my blindness why I couldn't let love win. If only I could believe that true love is built, lasting love eternally. It was my blinded perception of love and I constantly wanted to give up and die. Love spoke hope so I wouldn't stop in my pain; or curse His name in vain. Love gave me strength when I reflected on the turmoil's that has been. Love gave me hugs of comfort when I was alone and didn't want to let anyone in. I am the love without questioning, what, to the end; I'm Jesus, covering all filthy sin; Giving signs and wonders; giving you authority to fight to win…Only to those, I trust and know that my words sunk in; releasing church ministry on ever end. To those that love and obey me; I give them my love so they can continue to believe that I am He, that sit on the right side of Father God and intercede. Love is me. I died so your being can live and be free. Looking at your skin; it's my hope that you see you're perishable without my light. Here's my Grace, persevering life. I also have Mercy for your blinded eye. I love you, that is what love is to life.

I was caged. I saw life through shackled bars. I had no control over my emotions. I could not see beyond my fears. Those same problems grew in the cracks of love, peace, joy, trust, and acceptance. I could not love anyone correctly because I didn't love myself. Oddly enough though, I thought I was loving myself. I did not have a problem with my physical appearance; I was on the verge of being overly confident in myself; conceded. I could stand being alone and laughing with myself. I also used my helping hand to others to defuse my inner brokenness. I knew if I prayed for others God would hear it. I've seen my prayers answered for others many, many times. Why? Because I believed in the life I was speaking into. Crazy that I couldn't do it for myself. I had blockage; even more so I believed God hated me; but Loved others. I stopped church again.

In 2016, moving into 2017, I still couldn't let love win. My heart was stopped; stuck at gunpoint; traveling through the odd years of comprehended love. I was being tricked by the enemy in every which way. Literally! I trusted the dark pits of night with light. My car was stolen; however, I had two, so I hopped in the other one. I was hit by a car; and burned my left leg on the tire. I was forced out of a car in the middle of a highway with no stable mind. I stopped going to school and work because I wanted to hide and shield my pains…. and there was my Delise, trying her best to relieve me the best she knew. However, I went back and still slept with the enemy! Later, I got served with protection papers. My mind was blown; I had literally just slept with the dude and now I had to go to court and fight for my rights. After the hearing, I barely made it

outside. Soon as my face hit the air, I cried over the ramp…
feeling completely betrayed. Love was robbed from me.

As months passed, I attached myself back with a former
fling. I loved how he cared and catered to my known needs. I
could call and talk to him about anything. I was using him, and
he let me know it was alright... that he wanted to be used in any
way possible.

I remember Boo popped up at my front door grabbing
me stern, "Yanna get your life together. You need to go to
church." "No, I don't. You need to." His words echoed in my
head. I then felt embarrassed, because I have always been a
church goer, just never applied the resources to my life. Also,
he scared the life out of me, my hook up had just departed
within seconds of his arrival. After Boo embraced me; it was the
look in his eyes that showed a high level of care and concern or
maybe another hidden agenda. I didn't know my trust was shot.

Bruised Me

"It's your fault!"

"Who me?"

"Yeah you! You left me! I loved you and never wanted you to leave! I told you."

"So, you blame me? I told you to go, but you wouldn't leave me. I was tired of fighting for you, so it was time to do me. I love you, that's why I'm here, standing in your door! You can see."

"Well hello to me. You bruised me and my heart skipped many beats."

"I'm sorry, but I was fighting for peace."

"I was unhealthy looking for the star in me; but you knew I love you. You bruised me."

"Show me your bruise… let me see."

"No!"

"Are you sure it was me. I carried you until I got weak. I'm back now… I'm asking that you give

God your Yes for me."

"Only if you leave; … wait don't go I need you, please."

I was coming into grips that I didn't want to hurt anymore; but it became even more hurtful because I didn't know where to begin. I knew "of" God, but I didn't know how to Trust God. Plus, I was battling with un-forgiveness. I didn't operate in hate, but love. However, trust! … Which then grew me to just lust. I felt like I needed to be held and penetrated; but I was smart enough to realize that I didn't want anymore bodies. It was easy to fall back into convenience.

Going to church came with conviction. The Word was being brought forward to heal me; I could not receive it. But I continued to seek God and he actually came to me; I turned from him because I didn't feel worthy of his presence; and also, because I was comfortable in survival mode because it's what I knew. I was fighting battles that were already won.

Though I was trying to get out of my own head and become a healthy adult; my best friend Cam and his girlfriend were murdered. My spirit was troubled because I couldn't fathom that I was experiencing more losses. Also, Wesley, a former boyfriend, was murdered days within Cam's. My heart kept breaking before it was repaired!

Dilemma

Summa Sixteen!

Friends getting left laid in the struggle,

Breaking hearts in a double. A double homicide.

Another part of me vanished and died.

The level of guilt was deeply felt. You told me that you were thankful for me. Searching for peace is the only thing keeping me. You were my guy; I was proud of you for pushing through trying to beat the odds. When you died, it took my mental like a soul tie. I close my eyes and my heart still cry. I close my eyes and still see blood cry. Questioning the in-betweens of repeated hurts of Why! Stop the wet pain from running down my eyes. Summa sixteen what a double homicide.

Doubtful

God I gotta choose you.

I don't wanna die and never know the truth,

As to;

Where you reside;

And if I'll live after this life.

My life seems to be based on a lie;

I can't possibly have dreams waiting;

inside, ALIVE.

Help me to trust you.

Can you use my vessel?

I'm still doubtful.

Well

Purified Lea!
Do you believe
London's river by the bay?
No, oppression has to stay.
God ushers Grace:
Mercy to stay.
Favor, is that you?
It's Lea,
Green pastures of stay.
I heard if I made it to the well;
My pains of yesterday, pulled in day,
Won't have a place to stay.
Well!
Are you by the bay of green pastures of stay?
God, is it You for me,
Waiting in the deep wells where dirt always had a place to be!
Lord if you should take the dirt, pushing clay.
Take my burdens of yesterday, replacing leaps of joy in
TODAY.

I welcomed in the New Year at Living Water Fellowship Church: Pastor Kim; Sunday, January 1, 2017. "Is that you? Raise your hand." Every word that Pastor Kim spoke that day was, indeed, me. I was broken and confused. I needed the healing that only God could have brought. I became an active member joining the intercessors and usher board. Upon my meeting with the intercessors, they expressed how we must be truthful with who we are in order to be in position to help others. There I stood embarrassed and ashamed to admit that I was being immoral, and smoking weed to numb the heart aches. I never spoke of my pains and brokenness. However, I expressed my known flaws openly. I stopped smoking weed and having sex. Though I stopped having sex; guess what… you guessed it! I was already pregnant. As soon as I found out, I told leadership I was with child; because I knew the importance of being honest while being in position to lead others.

I indeed was embarrassed because I was practicing abstinence; being whole and complete. I remember Pastor Kim speaking on satisfaction shortly afterwards. I was extremely emboosticated. I went from leading in ministry to sitting in the pupils. I wanted to explain my story to all the eyes watching. Though I was shutting down; I never stopped going to church. I dealt with the humiliation and my present condition outside of church. No one really knew I was suffering inside. How I went from having my own apartment and car to losing it all… to buying a beater; because I was in the way of God plans…

I was sleeping on folks' couch openly, being looked at as mediocre. I had to ignore the hate, or someone was going to die. I had a lot and range hidden in me. I operated in love; but seeing certain people and watching their body language... I was ready to strike. I had to ignore the misconception and hate... I had to remain focused. I did so by going to entrepreneur meetings: women empowerment groups, a few radio stations, to church on Sundays: midweek on Wednesdays, and work throughout the week.

Marguerite Press

I prayed over my stomach and asked God to give me the strength to run the race. I was tired and ready to flash out; but I knew my time was limited to be in that condition. I had to remind myself why I was in that predicament; I put myself there. I was just grateful that Jesus was still with me.

During the summer of 2017, I worked at Living Water Fellowship Church Outreach. I was awarded to be the Youth Director working with Mrs. Deborah. Oddly, enough Mrs. Deborah knew both of my parents. I wasn't sure about the dept of their relationship; but she looked at me and said I know your dad and mom. I was blown; okay. Any who; while dragging into work; I felt defeated. I was tired, because I never was able to get adequate sleep; plus, I was pregnant, growing by the day.

However, one day, while working, I was sitting thinking of the baby's name. I wasn't sure what I was having, but my spirit broke and confirmed I was having a girl. I wrote down many names; Leilani stood out the most. I had no idea what it meant at the time; but I soon learned. Leilani: Heavenly Flowers. I was instantly emotional. Later, I saw my baby girl's face; just round and full. She looked exactly like I envisioned post birth.

My pregnancy with Leilani was nothing easy. I had to swallow blood from my busted lip. I had to gasp for air after choking hands, releasing me to the cold outdoors. I also watched a so-called friend walk past me knowing I felt helpless. Crazy I loved the chick and her brother. Anyhow, I was sick from the time I found out that I was pregnant. Giving life to my sweet girl; it almost cost me mine. I had to get iron infusions on the regular to remain healthy.

If truth be told, if it weren't for my mother popping in and connecting with me while I was pregnant with Leilani; I doubt she or I would have been here. My mom carried my birthing pains when she could. My mother was the one who actually told me I was pregnant. With my face all turned up in denial, I denied the notification; until reality hit and I realized I had missed my cycle. My mom gave me my first baby gift and said, "Now, I'll be there when you have her" … and she indeed was.

My mother was the first visitor while I was in labor and delivery. All of my outside support failed me. I had to catch an uber to the hospital to make my delivery appointment. My mom called and yelled, "I'm on my way!". Still to this day, I have no idea how my mom knew I was in labor and delivery. My mom kept her word that day, no matter her condition. I knew then that my mom really loved me; and if she had the strength and the mindset to beat the odds, she would.

January 30th, of 2018, Boo came to support our beloved princess birthing: my cousin showed up; Joy Bells, my brother Rasheed, and my pops. Lord Jesus take the wheel. I don't even want to tell yawl the rest. In summary, I was seconds away from not making back to this life. Leilani was a high-risk pregnancy. My life was high risk.

I just knew God was tired of Gracing me; but I was at the hands of the mercy seat... He wasn't done with me yet. I knew Jesus' Spirit. I felt the Holy Spirit temporarily at Living Water Fellowship for the first time in my life! And before that I could always sense the Holy Spirit, but would never welcome Him in. Any who, Naomi came, my Favorite Big Sister Moni came bearing love gifts, and my baby cousin.

After being released from the hospital; I had the pleasure of walking into my warm, clean, furnished home with food. Naomi helped me. What a blessing she was. However, after all the excitement about new life calmed down, I was left dealing with me. I felt empty and alone; but I understood why God allowed my Leilani Flower; my pleasant delight: Delise, to be born in that season; she was my birthing gift. When I saw my baby, I knew I had to put an end to the generational curse. Lei'Day was my Grace baby giving me back some joy and youth. She was so peaceful like an angel sent from Heaven. Though she had her dad's face, she reflected me. The girl could eat too. I had to stop giving her the boob because she was ripping my skin; trying to get to all the substance she could hold. I wanted to nurse her like I did for big brother, D3; however, I still pumped. ...Sooner than later my Aunt came to fill the voids of discomfort.

Trust Mee

You're not alone,

You just don't trust me and won't hold on. I called you by name... But you're so busy that you didn't hear…So, go on. You'll be back… because without me your possibilities are lack. Causing burdens to hold on. Only if you could see; what my Father has for you to be! No mediocrity: it's pure… more than the food you eat.

     Only one out of my three aunts come over. It was the very aunt that I made up in my mind to forgive. After all I loved her and missed her. I allowed her to embrace the freshness of my home. It also was a joy to see her beauty and smell her rich perfume. It didn't take long before I was bamboozled again. Aunty bought my baby girl and beautiful crystal bracelet and gave me a ring liken to the very one she was wearing. She then brought me a rock and expressed how it pulls out negative energy and once it cracks you have to put it in the sunlight to recharge. Naive I was! Those same demonic spirits were trying to attach themselves to my brokenness. She bought me a glass mixer etc. I was looking passed the pull of being sucked back into Buddhism.

     On February 16th of 2018, a few weeks after my birthday, I bought myself a Mustang and ditched my Nissan. The next day, I drove down to Fort Wayne, IN. The joy it was to bring my babies together as one; it eased the pain I was experiencing from my surgery and my mental state. Fort Wayne started to be my saving Grace. Apostle Oscar J. Nelson Dowdell-Underwood Jr. Ph.D. was pouring life into me; not only was he teaching me, but he gave me the tools and strategies. "Ayanna, God knows you." In that moment I felt a rush that was more than an emotion. It was like my soul was being snatched out and uplifted in a place of safety. Apostle drilled the importance of gratitude and how to keep a heart of love. Keeping a heart of love to folks that tried their hardest to destroy me subliminally, was extremely hard. I wanted to express my pains in detail without feeling like a victim, and making folks feel sorry for me. However, my story was a sad song.

As I reflect back to the summer of 2017, I was weak. I allowed the devil to use me. Honoring persons that constantly reminded you of the pain and struggle you no longer wanted to be a part of seemed impossible. I fought Pops, the very man that I always feared. I was reminded constantly that I was powerless and that without his guidance and me honoring him; I wouldn't live long. Trying to honor a man that was self-righteous, unforgiving, controlling, and pure evil was painful. Though I knew these things to be true; I wanted to learn how to love the hell out of him and forgive him completely so that my life could move forward.

However, I watched him beat on people and I knew for sure I wasn't going to be another number. I was listening to the ill words that were expressed through a man that I longed for, caused me to provoke the enemy. Instead of leaving as I should have; I turned and faced him… "I'm not a little girl anymore and you will respect me!" I demanded respect and let him know that I was no longer afraid of him. I was no longer going to listen to him degrade and bash me without taking a stance.

"You look like a hoodrat. You diking. You lucky I didn't fuck you; you know how many father's fuck their daughters!" .... That verbal abuse of toxicity extended, never ending in love and appreciation of my being. All along, I was stopping by so I could help with his needs. I had a car again and had in mind to let him take a spin, like he did the previous day.

The very man that I wanted to put my trust in betrayed me. I couldn't trust him with my pains. He would bring up my wounds and use them against me. He told everyone that spoke highly of me or showed interest in my being that I was a major hinderance: problem.

I was embarrassed about who my father was. Why? Because I saw that man as a reflection of me. I watched how he played with God and the anointing over and over. He even went as far as setting up church in our home to lure women and to set up disagreements. He would read a scripture to me then cuss me out; not only was I confused, but I also grew angry. Here I was trying to forgive pops from past failures, and he dug deeper in my wounds he helped create. I remember watching him send the tray around pretending that he had a congregation. I put my last in only to watch him take it and buy cigarettes with it after his shindig. In summary, everything was slipping.

Our childhood domains were no longer in the possession of Mr. Tipton. Gone! Winthrop was now state property. The state gave him a notice to pack up and hit the hay. I remember pops and another lady that he considered a prophetess or evangelist; whatever, came and prophesied that his house would not be foreclosed, and that Winthrop was a holy land. Humm. Yeah about a few weeks later, a big dump truck sat in the very driveway that pops had laid down before taking care of our essentials. I can't lie, it still pained me to see my dad not surrender and honor that he had to leave his home; even more so to see childhood memories flash before me.

My mom again, out of the blew appeared. I took pictures as my mommy kneeled by my dad's side and loved on him. Her smile was still pleasant. Her eyes still had fighting life; bright and radiant. Her heart cared for the very man the rippled hers apart.

As a kid I saw my pops like dude in The Color Purple: Danny Glover. I'm like if this evil man doesn't change his ways, he's going to live a lonely life, and when he needs help, he may just have to find a new body to use; because his known helpers were burnt out; but Grace..... Then there's little oh me that never gave up and kept reaching. Each time I got my fingers chopped off, then my arms... Now my legs could still move, and my heart had not failed me. I still had love to give.

Ephesians helped clear out the confusing. I just knew my days were ending. I felt like I just completely disobeyed my dad; and of course, lacked honor. My heart was broken. My intentions were to simply repair my brokenness from previous years; not to come and cause more harm because I lacked self-control and my emotions were not settled. I wanted to build a healthy relationship with my dad; especially since my personal relationship with my children's dad kept failing in cycles.

Family Relationships: Ephesians 6: 1-4

Children obey your parents in the Lord [that is, accept their guidance and discipline as His representatives], for this is right [for obedience teaches wisdom and self-discipline]. Honor [esteem, value as precious] your father and your mother [and be respectful to them]—this is the first commandment with a promise— so that it may be well with you, and that you may have a long life on the earth. Fathers, do not provoke your children to anger [do not exasperate them to the point of resentment with demands that are trivial or unreasonable or humiliating or abusive; nor by showing favoritism or indifference to any of them], but bring them up [tenderly, with loving-kindness] in the discipline and instruction of the Lord.

It Wasn't Easy

The hand that rocked the cradle; fatal, attraction to the lost hopes with no trace of the promised land to humanity. It wasn't easy walking through the storms with no substance to hold on. I was feeding pigs with my feet. I gave my heart to flesh, a set defeat. The stains of pain made me live life in the rain. Even tornados came, but somehow, I didn't get swallowed up, the Son came. "Ayanna I'm keeping watch, in my Father's name." I still lost sight. I kept seeing burning houses on Winthrop, but only one going up in flames. Seeing weeds living longer than the beauty in flowers caused great PAIN. It wasn't easy hearing screams being falsified Jesus' name.

Reflection

A reflection of you, of me; and me of you.

But who are you? Only if you knew…...

Bruised knees still could move.

DONT stop and stand stiff.

Focus on the Truth that attest.

It's in the dirt, that your true beauty exists!

Not all sparkles are seen,

But missed.

It was the reflection that I turned and kissed.

Love Inside

…. Never give up on Love; because Love will never give up on you. Don't get blinded by the feelings, rooting emotions trying to cover inside. If God is love; then it's Love that's still Alive. Love inside… Gotta speak to the soul that paralyzed. Love on the inside, kissing bondage goodbye. Love on the inside, uprooting generational defeat. Love on the inside will remove your feet from poverty. Never give up on LOVE; because it's He that wants you to Win…. Above. Let love win inside; locked deep, poisoning the outside….. Never give up on love; because love will never give up on you. Don't get blinded by the feelings; rooting emotions trying to cover inside. If God is love; then it's Love that's still Alive. Love inside… poisoning the outside.

Back to 2018…... God prepared a Man of God that would help me to later trust and depend on Jesus Christ. A man that would speak life to dying bones. A man that was full of Grace. A man that feared the Lord and taught nothing but the truth. A man that understood, when to speak and when not to. A man! A man! A man… that taught me that Father God was nothing like our Earthly fathers. A man that gave unselfishly. A man that encouraged his congregation to cover each other with the love of Jesus. A man that would leave the ninety-nine to go after the one with love. A man that will guide us by the Word and love when we are about to self-destruct. A man that taught possibilities: My beloved Pastor, Leader, Teacher, Prophet, Grandfather, Dad; Apostle, Oscar J. Nelson Dowdell-Underwood Jr. Ph.D.

Deuteronomy 18: 15 "The LORD your God will raise up for you a prophet like me [Moses] from among you, from your countrymen (brothers, brethren). You shall listen to him.

1 Timothy 3: 1-7 1 This is a faithful *and* trustworthy saying: if any man [eagerly] seeks the office of [a]overseer (bishop, superintendent), he desires an excellent task. 2Now an overseer must be blameless *and* beyond reproach, the husband of one wife, self-controlled, sensible, respectable, hospitable, able to teach, 3not addicted to wine, not [b]a bully *nor* quick-tempered *and* hot-headed, but gentle *and* considerate, free from the love of money [not greedy for wealth and its inherent power--financially ethical]. 4*He must* manage his own household well,

keeping his children under control with all dignity [keeping them respectful and well-behaved] 5(for if a man does not know how to manage his own household, how will he take care of the church of God?). 6 and *He must* not be a new convert, so that he will not [behave stupidly and] become conceited [by appointment to this high office] and fall into the [same] condemnation incurred by the devil [for his arrogance and pride]. 7And he must have a good reputation and be well thought of by those outside the church, so that he will not be discredited and fall into the devil's trap.

….. My Pastor!!! I assure. Yes sir. All day; ain't that right Lei 'Day… Day Day! D3 you know: Follow Your Dreams and someday you'll make it to the top: For only on top…. Gotta get to C-Prep to get the rest. Cornerstone: Ft. Wayne.

2018, was a major shift for me. I had not yet come to grips that I was the only one stopping my forward processing. Here, I am now with two children and still no husband. I was embarrassed for repeating the same cycle; and leaving a whole in my heart. It was never ideal for me to be a single mother; after all I wanted to be a wife and have a healthy family. But did I know what it took to become a wife? Was I whole? Or still broken looking for sympathy and validation? Did I understand the process of singleness? Have I become one with God; trusting Jesus to deliver me and quicken my spirit?

Wifey

Stop looking for me;

I am your husband, but let me be.

Let me come to you in peace.

Just be whole and ready for me.

It was the strong presence of the Holy Spirit that opened my trust to the man of God, Dr. Oscar J. Nelson Dowdell-Underwood Jr., Ph.D. Pastor spoke life to my dying, dried out bones. Due to my lack of belief of knowing that I was possible in Christ; allowed me to hear my Apostle, but not believe. I wanted my pastor to just heal me already, not knowing that it was a process. Apostle was authorized to teach and instruct me. He was incredibly careful about his position in leadership. Never once did my Apostle not acknowledge God first, showing utmost respect to the body of Christ. I found my healing through His teachings. It was God, through my apostle that healed, taught, and instructed me.

I love that my pastor does not discriminate among persons. He operates in pure love, in the accordance of the trinity. I knew my Apostle was an honorable man of God because I asked God about him. It wasn't long after that the Holy Spirit greeted me through my Apostle and spoke directly to me, giving me direct confirmation and revelation. It was so easy to question how long the Holy Spirit would be with my Apostle because I had been let down by other pastors, and I needed Jesus himself to validate this one and He did, introducing me to the fivefold ministry.

Unity of the Spirit

So, I, the prisoner for the Lord, appeal to you to live a life worthy of the calling to which you have been called [that is, to live a life that exhibits godly character, moral courage, personal integrity, and mature behavior—a life that expresses gratitude to God for your salvation], with all humility [forsaking self-righteousness], and gentleness [maintaining self-control], with patience, bearing with one another [a]in [unselfish] love. Make every effort to keep the oneness of the Spirit in the bond of peace [each individual working together to make the whole successful]. There is one body [of believers] and one Spirit— just as you were called to one hope when called [to salvation]— one Lord, one faith, one baptism, one God and Father of us all who is [sovereign] over all and [working] through all and [living] in all. Yet grace [God's undeserved favor] was given to each one of us [not indiscriminately, but in different ways] in proportion to the measure of Christ's [rich and abundant] gift.

~ Ephesians 4 1-7

~ Ephesians 11-13

And [His gifts to the church were varied and] He Himself appointed some as apostles [special messengers, representatives], some as prophets [who speak a new message from God to the people], some as evangelists [who spread the good news of salvation], and some as pastors and teachers [to shepherd and guide and instruct], [12] [and He did this] to fully equip *and* perfect the saints (God's people) for works of service, to build up the body of Christ [the church]; [13] until we all reach oneness in the faith and in the knowledge of the Son of God, [growing spiritually] to become a mature believer, reaching to the measure of the fullness of Christ [manifesting His spiritual completeness and exercising our spiritual gifts in unity].

The Destiny Dome Embassy @ Cathedral of Praise Int. an I Am Possible Grace Church under direction of Apostle, Dr. Oscar J. Nelson Dowdell-Underwood Jr. Senior Pastor. I tried my hardest to master my abilities and see what my Apostle saw in me. "Stop worrying about what others think of you." To my deceptive mind, I thought I didn't care about what others thought. However, as I thought some more, I realized that I did care. However, it was a confusing process. I hated being misunderstood; but I guess it wasn't my job to explain. I was ready to fight; but not in the manner that my Apostle was teaching… street fight; that ratchet, ghetto mentality that seems to control my temperament when folk misunderstood.

Due to the challenges and discomfort, I was experiencing in this time of my life, getting up and going to church became hard… I knew I wanted to change my life and live out the fullness of my. God-given destiny. However, while I was sick the enemy constantly reminded me of my struggle. I paid more attention to the negativity and my struggles. I so desperately wanted to get ratchet and strike. However, no matter how I felt or what I was dealing with in my personal life, it was necessary for me to make it to The Dome. My Apostle has a way of shifting my atmosphere led by Holy Spirit, every single time.

I never left church the way I came in. I will admit, I was weak and still needed to grow. At any point in my life should I have ever been worried about what others were saying or thinking about me. Again, my Apostle, told me not to worry. I was stuck on survivor mode.

So, in summary, my heart started growing cold; but Pastor kept reminding on every encounter to keep a heart of love; and to have a Gratitude; HONOR. ...and to keep the FAITH in God and have Mercy. … the same Mercy that was given to me repeatedly.

I was really humiliated if I must say, my private life was being leaked through the very persons I was trusting. More times than not, it was false information getting leaked: of course, some truths but not nearly all. I hated it. I wanted to validate the truth; but instead, I grew numb and limited communication. Again, I tried my hardest to follow the instructions of my Apostle. "Keep a heart of love." "GRATITUDE" "HONOR" … Keep FAITH in God. Have MERCY.

I, Ayanna Lea Tipton, hardheaded. The Lord helped me though…. The word definitely speaks on how we should not grieve the Holy Spirit. You'll find that in Ephesians 4:30. How I was feeling inwards was affecting my health majorly. I remember my back side burning with sharp pain; first appearing red and later blistering bumps. The surface hurt to touch…... Whew! Painful. I was so embarrassed that I had shingles the day of my son's honor ball. I was so uncomfortable. I didn't want to ruin my son's days, so I bit the bullet; and of course, I was pressed this day by the enemy as well.

Rewinding back, DDE@COPI was the very church Boo brought me too in 2012. As I walked to be seated, all eyes were on me. Later February 3rd of 2013, Pastor dedicated my son,

D3 back to the Lord. The eyes never stopped. I reappeared in 2016 for Deep Wells; and that was the second time I felt the Holy Spirit, and Pastor told me God forgave me. I was blown away. I couldn't fathom… that Jesus loved me; maybe other persons, but not me. I didn't understand why my Apostle said that God forgave me… As

I had the Grace to continue to live; I knew exactly why my Apostle released those words to my ear gates. God was helping my Apostle speak life in my dry bones; but these bones had been dried for so long… it took a lot of work!

Now, fast forwarding to the return of 2018, I was stuck in a hard place. I had just given birth to my baby girl and I didn't know which way to go. My money was coming in heavy,

112

I had a new car, and crib; but I was even sadder than when I was living paycheck to paycheck. I didn't understand why I felt so emptied out when I gained more money and could provide for my babies alone. I then got extremely depressed. I was driving back and forward, up and down the highway.

January 30th, 2018, my Leilani Delise was presented back to the Lord by Apostle, Oscar J. Nelson Dowdell-Underwood Jr. I was so emotional that day. I was battling with DNA results, though the birth certificate was already signed. It pained me to have various faces of distant family, surround my baby's dedication for various reasons, but no matter what, I knew my baby girl was protected and Jesus took full ownership. Around June of 2018, I had to make the decision if I was going back to work or if I was moving to Fort Wayne. A part of me wanted to fly back to Fort Wayne, because I knew there was a shield of protection around my church domains. I wanted to keep my Apostle in my pocket. I felt like I couldn't live without him; however, he taught me later I could. Moreover, the other part of me did not want to leave my new apartment behind; but I did. I packed up and moved to Fort Wayne.

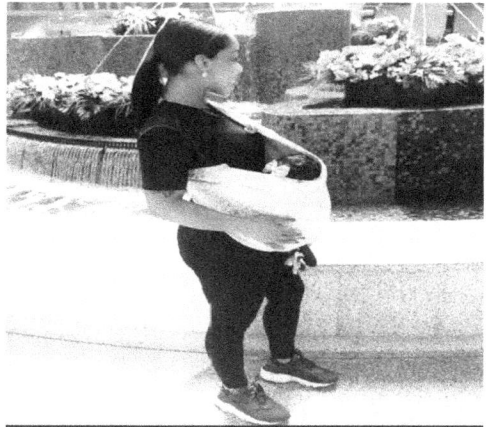

I was attracted to the Word. I loved the style and the manner that the Word was being brought forward by my

Apostle. I could see through my Apostle and get a true connection with the Holy Spirit. Of course, I had to return home and fight my demons. I would just shut myself in the room. I was constantly reminded of being that broken impaired little girl. The more I reflected over my life, all I could see is that I would never make it out of this life reaching the fullness of my GOD-given destiny. The more I tried to release pain; the more vivid memories and voices of defeat came.

"Do not remember the former things or ponder the things of the past. "Listen carefully, I am about to do a new thing, now it will spring forth; Will you not be aware of it? I will even put a road in the wilderness. Rivers in the desert. ~Isaiah 43:18-19

When you don't follow instructions, this is what happens… I began getting anxiety again. I couldn't deal with the clutter circling my life. I like to have everything in order. I then started smoking weed again. I was angry with myself for not having a plan and not being patient before I jumped on the highway to move. Apostle was teaching on honor. I knew what honor was, but I didn't know in what manner I was supposed to use it. My little self-accepted the mic one Sunday morning and told the church how thankful I was for my Apostle, for teaching me how to honor people. When I think of that; I'm in disbelief. I was full of pain. I just spoke my truth.

After going to church, I questioned myself to see if I was being dishonorable and the root of my own problems. I was lost at this point; completely confused. I knew what love was now because I was being taught; however, I felt defeated because I only felt love at church; through my Apostle… and other members.

Though my Apostle told me not to worry about what others think, I couldn't do anything but focus on their thoughts. I wanted to tell my story. Almost every Sunday, the Holy Spirit was grabbing hold on me. I have never been the person that liked to cry in front of people; let alone stand, lift and hand to give God thanks… but it was that Word of conviction and Truth that kept me out of my seat. I was thankful that the Holy Spirit was speaking to current situations through my pastor. Apostle stayed being spot on with the message from God.

My Apostle was watering the flowers in Ayanna. Ayanna means beautiful flower, well-spring, and innocent, also colored vegetables.

Sounds pretty healthy to me; if only I could trust and believe I was a flower and no weed. I had the opportunity to minister through dance at church. I wanted to dance to break free. I still had shackled bars. My mind scared me. However, I found myself in low dark places. I just wanted to express myself through movement.

I knew dancing would help defuse the enemy; so, I could break free. It's me that can dance to any beat without memory. I just wanted to praise and grow strong. I wanted to go to a new place with no hindrance, even if I was causing it or if I was allowing myself to be hinder by the opinions of others. I just desire be in a place where I can be my best me and worship.

August 12th of 2018, "I made up in my life a long time ago, I wasn't going to focus on what I didn't have. I learned a long time ago, Ayanna! I give how I wanna live…. Because there's something about a seed; as long as the earth remains: seedtime, and harvest will not stop. I (You)can give my way to the life I (You) dream. Lift your hand up. But the enemy wants you to be so mesmerized, you didn't give me as much as you gave them."

Genesis 8: 22

"While the earth remains,

Seedtime and harvest,

Cold and heat,

Winter and summer,

And day and night

Shall not cease."

I have always been a giver; especially if I had what that person needed. I love giving to people that poured into me; rather rich or poor. It was a level of high respect and done out of pure love. I also like to give just in general. I enjoy seeing people laugh and smile; and even cry in joy. I learned over the years; to give freely; not expecting nothing in return from the gift. Give out of complete love... and it'll be given back. Though I was a giver, I still had not yet mastered; nor healed from the wounding of my past. On December 1, 2019, Apostle spoke, "Ayanna we have to figure out the chaos that's been called your life."

Fostered Mind

Fostered with lost care, my mind isn't my own. I'm being controlled by past failures; I hold on. Mind over matter... Gravity appears. Releasing the door that holds my future near. Prosperity you seemed so close: BUT, fear... Extended the distance of a seasonal year. Matter of you; you matter. Mind why you foster me? I already fought through bruised knees. Walking on water almost drowned me; I lacked faith you see. In this life, I learned that a fostered mind is a dot in dark times. Fostered mind, bow and give God your knees. If I have to crawl, so my family to friends can see... Then gravity, it's time to find the key that meets, so potential can be more than hope; but a dream lived to see. Yes, I know I need faith; to believe. To Every Yes, that Eases False Dreams, replacing Eyeing Yesterday's Evils, that holds Dreams. Fostered mind, you no longer foster me; I hear you knocking, but you don't have the key that meets.

The level of pain was submerging me; but God stayed with me and brought help. I had angels of protection. Though I had no kinfolks in Fort Wayne, IN; I had family: Momma D and my sister's Nae and E. Momma D ushered in the long love lost. Momma D became a mother for me. I absolutely love her!! Love her. She prepared meals of comfort; laughs of joy; cozy home; with plenty of room to heal broken hearts. Thanks, My

Momma D. ... and yes! The enemy tried to destroy that connection too. Ask em' did it work!

Momma D helped me find a place to live where I could grow and develop. "Remember what Pastor said Yanna," "Never despise small beginnings." "Easter you're going to be just fine." 512 E., best known as the waiting room! I absolutely hated the outside; location was okay; but the foundation before entertaining into my studio dampened my spirits. "Gratitude! AYANNA!"

Note to self: Be thankful for peace. You prayed and God brought an urgent shift of light, through Jesus Christ.

February 5, 2019, had my own place; with little to no income. I didn't feel safe sending my baby to childcare, but I managed. June 9th of 2019, it's by the Grace of God, that I received my Associates of Arts in Christian Business degree. I did not have to worry about how I was going to pay for college, God made away. I was able to afford

my school fees' and I also was able to finish the assignment!
My babies were present supporting me; Ms. Naomi supported
me, and others. My feelings weren't to hurt this time. I had
some substance to hold. My Apostle was telling me that a
degree means nothing… it's not about a piece of paper… that
paper isn't who you are. It's more so off the paper and what
you do and become.

July 5th of 2019, my son left before his sister and I to
Texas. It pained me deeply to watch my son depart from me
again. It felt like open heart surgery without anesthesia.
However, it was necessary. Shortly afterwards, Boo put me on
my first flight as an adult, and second in lifetime to Orlando
Florida. My D3 and Leilani flowers were reunited.

As the months grew; I felt the need to be where the boys
were. I was so anxious to be where they were. After visiting
Dallas in January, within a few days; I drove to Texas from Fort
Wayne, Indiana. However, I made it. I didn't plan it all out. All I
knew was my lease was up on February fifth of 2020 … I took
a leap of faith, not knowing the ends and out. Crazy to say I
took a leap of faith, because I had a hard time trusting Jesus
with my life. I had a hard time believing that I'll one day be the
person I dreamed to be. I remember asking God to help me
with my decisions; I wasn't still enough to hear. My mind was
already set on go. My bag was already packed.

After getting sick, I learned I was pregnant. The visit to Texas, before the move, met conception. I made it to 7 months. D4 passed July 16th of 2020. He was delivered at 9:55 am. He weighed 2lbd, 4.8oz; and was 13.78 inches long. My room number was B3555. God is international and so AM I. My Apostle sent a word, and those words went in the depths of my inner cord. Pastor told me, "Ayanna, you're going to be just fine." I mean, Pastor was just as calm as can be. My Apostle was coaching me through my pains. After hearing his restful state, I was then able to snap back to reality; though the pain didn't stop. I then began to catch grip as to why God allowed my baby to return to him before his eyes opened; however, I felt still; unmovable.

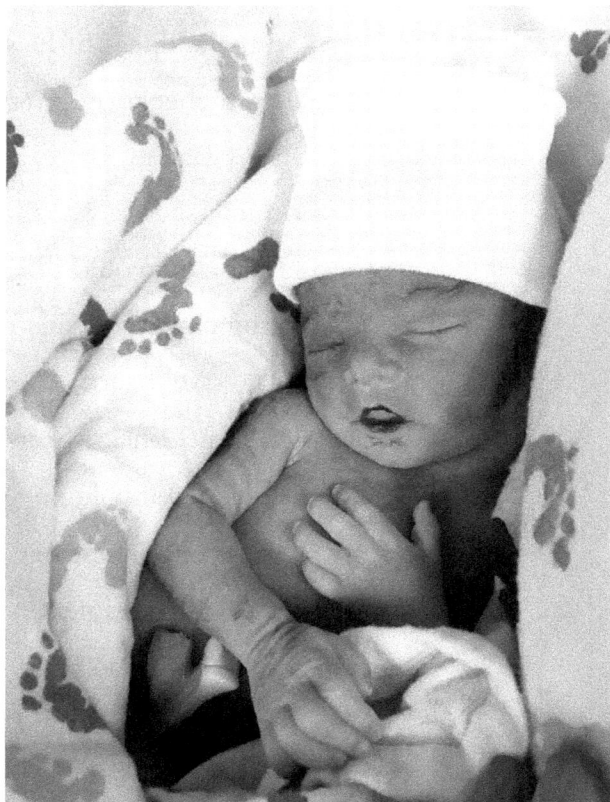

Still 7

In the stillness of Day,

I kissed cold cheeks, hoping for life.

Mommy waited for your cry;

but nothing; silence was the reply.

God knew July, would Still Seven;

bringing closure to sins high.

My heart;

I wanted to hear heart beats to life;

See shadows of beaming light.

Heaven, Still Seven;

Bringing Divine completion to eyes.

Not being able to hold you to keep you warm,

…Is where my Destiny Drive.

Still 7,

Kissing Heaven;

I'm thankful you're Alive.

My beloved Uncle Jasper and his beautiful wife supported me from the time I made it to Dallas, Texas. They also stood by my side in the hospital. My precious Aunt Renee even went through the limits to bring unconditional love and comfort. I am truly thankful for your high regards of honor. Your meekness and cleanliness; I paid close attention too. Can't no filth tell me about my beloved Aunt Renee. I'm blackening er' ten toes. I love you unconditional Queen. I will seek prayer for you daily. Love you always: Blessed and Highly Favored you are. I can't thank you enough for your acceptance of me. My baby girl loves you unconditionally as well. D3 enjoys your best dishes. You capitalize Queen. Love you tons.

After long hours at work, my uncle-cousin came bearing more love with gifts. He always tells me, "You have caviar taste, with sardine money." This is true; well for now anyways. I absolutely love when he says that, because that tells me that he knows I like quality; I must become so I can stay out of his pockets. I love my Uncle Jasper and Aunt Renee. My Uncle Jasper fought for our country and led other great men. A true leader and man that taught discipline; and how to process order. I'm grateful for you all. My heartbeats.

Back to room B355, I waited to hear my baby cry; but I never did. I felt so lost! Incomplete. Devastated. Embarrassed. Less of a Woman. Angry. Bitter. Numb. Dead. Sleep. I blamed everyone around me! "It's your fault!!! Especially my doctor. I couldn't stand to see his face. I had a million plus words for him. I had just left his office about three days prior going into labor. I was told everything was good and my baby was healthy. I kept asking, is my baby okay? I knew in my spirit that something was wrong; not necessarily wrong with my son; but I knew something was happening that was out of my control. Heartbeat was good! I could see my baby's face just fine on the ultrasound; but when the pictures were printed; NOPE. My baby was also breached, which was extremely weird for me. I kept trying to find reasons; to shape my high level of concern.

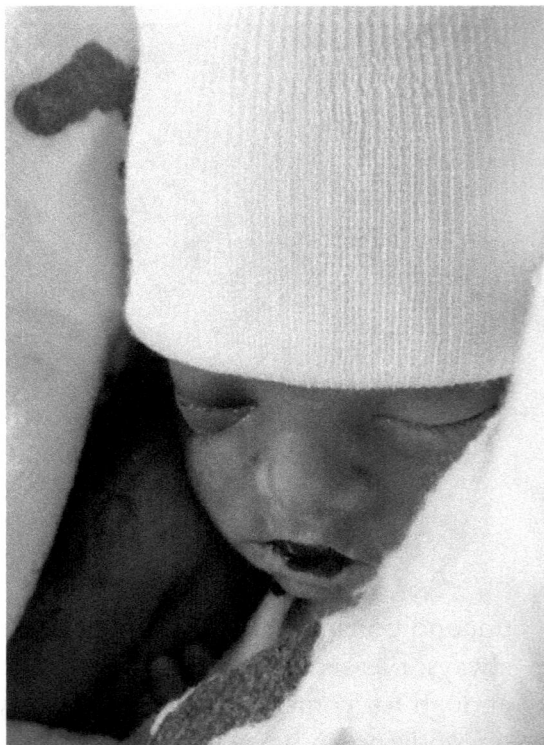

While in the hospital I had many praying for me. My friend Anthony, prayed with me every conversation. He had the members of his church also lifting me.

124

Upon leaving the hospital it felt like I was leaving something behind. I dreaded Boo rolling me out the hospital without our son; D4. Shortly afterwards, we were sitting at Allen Funeral home, preparing for our son's cremation. My body felt lifeless.

Within two weeks, I returned to Midway Rd to flowers from my employer: TruGreen. Seeing the flowers remind me of death instantly. My home: you could tell I had not been there. My beautiful plants died. My fish from TT were dead. Just death was reminded all around me. Though I was in pain. I cleaned! And brought life right back in my home. I cried every day; and Jesus came to me when I was on my balcony, "Ayanna, I love you that's why you have a baby in Heaven." It was a soft gentle voice, clear as the sky with no clouds. My God came and lifted the burden of guilt. I had miles of healing to travel through; but that helped me. Before I got home to a mass of funerals; on July 23 of 2020, while listening to my Apostle, he stated, "… Ayanna God still knows you!"

Light Fright

Red can't be go, but FIGHT.

Yellow Light…

Slow, but steady,

Yield! "God's Will,

Let me know when you're ready!"

Be patient! Trust God with you Life.

"I know you are strong; but this isn't your battle to fight!"

"Can, I cry. I'm feeling defeated and I can't question; because I know why."

Where's Green Light? Still running in the night.

Green is still Go, but fright.

Trust Green: Spring, and Go.

November 4th of 2020, I was arrested in my home for not being able to contain my feelings and emotions. I snapped! Though I snapped; this time I did not cause flesh to be broken and bleed. I did cause sore ears and sour eyes. However, due to lack of control and no flourishing fruit in "that" "moment," I was charged with AGG ASSAULT W/DEADLY WEAPON. My bond was set at 10,000.00, Cash or Surety. Ayanna Tipton; had felon written right by her name. I somehow still managed to smile when I got out; after I had a mental breakdown. I was thankful to be out on bond; but a part of me was broken. Seeing my baby's shoes; left footprints on my heart. Instead of becoming bitter and angry, I reverted to the sweet, calm, enjoyable; loveable woman I'm to be. I also threw every piece of clothing, to shoes in the trash that was worn to the facility.

The very night before I was arrested, I was talking to Naomi; expressing how I needed time away from everyone. I wasn't feeling healthy. I was sad that my son had just passed.

Then I learned my dad has stage four and cancer and his beloved sister's cancer cells sparked back up. I was done. My siblings and I had no healthy contact; expect my brother Jeffrey. He managed to make me smile. However, he was experiencing hell as well.

I wanted to be there for everyone; and I couldn't. I could feel the burdens of siblings and extended family. I never had time to just cry alone. I would shut myself in the closet and my babies would come find me. I'll sit out on the balcony and smoke weed and they would call for me. I needed serious help! From me losing my baby to getting locked up four months later really helped me to see who I was to God. It might not make sense to viewers; but perfect sense to me and the spiritual realm. "You don't have to fight the battle alone that God has already defeated for you. All you have to do as a believer is Trust the process."

As you all can see there's a pattern with weed. I put weed in the place of God. I grew weak in good doing and allowed the devil to consume my peace. To be honest, I never used weed just because…... My reasons since I smoked my first blunt was to feel numb; to escape the pain that I didn't want to talk about. Weed covered my fears and helped me to procrastinate and sleep. Weed helped dry my eyes. It relaxed me. Weed became my god.

…. I no longer use WEED as my God. God is more than temporary satisfaction; and in him I am able to defeat what seems impossible.

Jeremiah 29:11 "For I know the plans and thoughts that I have for you', says the Lord, 'plans for peace and well-being and not for disaster, to give you a future and a hope."

...Weeks later in November of 2020; I kept my smile.

Purposed'

... I still have fight in me,

More like a Light that kept life in me.

I could have easily chosen to hide and shield my pains and embarrassments from the world; but I decided there's a me out there blinded by the enemy. There's me out there scared to be free. There's a me out there that knows God and still falls short. I'm sharing my story in hopes to save someone's life… know that you matter. Know that God is a loving and forgiving God; and no matter where you are in life; you're reachable.

God test his beloved to see if we're ready for the life he has caused us to embrace. Oftentimes, believers forfeit; because the higher up… the more battles you have to face and overcome. However, know that you're never alone. In the darkest moments, life can be tricky… but hold fast to the living word. Don't let your mind drift off in a negative place. … and if your mind does drift off grab the holy bible and read any verse and believe every word. Then began giving God your thoughts. Ask God to cover your life and to give you understanding. Give him the wheel and the key, and just rest. Trust, you'll hear from Him. It's a small still voice; yet so loud and clear. Also, God can us anyone to bring what you lack; and allow you to see how possible you truly are in Him. Jesus will also teach you the most while you're alone. Why? So you can depend solely on Him; giving Father God all the Glory.

Allow your thoughts to be silent. Be still in God. For God is all knowing with all power in his hands. Though you may not feel like giving God your thoughts and heart… it's necessary! Please trust me. Avoiding your present help isn't worth the pain that God didn't intend for you. God gives us free will for a reason. Our free will separates the light from darkness. God tells us, "My people perish from a lack of knowledge." You must seek enlightenment in order to live a life that is pleasing to God; so that your deeds are considered finished and marked as good.

Know that every good deed isn't good. For example, it's good to feed the homeless; however, it isn't good if you're doing it for your own selfish reason…. though that man or woman, boy or girl may be blessed; your deed returns void to God, because you have become a master of yourself.

I've learned many things thus far in my 28 years of living; but the most important was choosing to depend on God. I'm thankful that no matter how I felt, I was able to find God; every time I sought for Him. "Seek and you shall find." I was able to speak life to my babies. I prayed with them and covered them. I made sure they were fed and bathed… have smiles of joy. I'm truly thankful for my babies because they gave me a reason to never give up! Really.

As I reflect, I remember wanting to give up and my babies would lift my head; bring me tissue and try to help me the best way possible. I hated that they ever saw me weak; but I am glad that my babies loved me enough to care for me when I didn't have the strength to do it for myself. "My children will grow up and call me blessed."

Depression, stress, and anxiety will sweep you off the map in 2.2. Understand that God knows we will fall short; that's what Jesus was created for; for you and me. Though I have spiritual insight, I'm not different than you or a non-believer. It takes choice every day to choose to be upright. To operate in this word with diligence, order, and obedience. Losing sight of God will have you searching for your freedom with binoculars never being able to see... until you come to grips that we are nothing without God: Jesus Christ; we will perish. We perish way faster without God.

One thing for certain, God will use when you think He can't. In your darkest hours, if you could just trust God, he will deliver you out of the hand of the fowler.

You look around at the world we live in today. The entertainers are only important because many can feel their story; they can relate. However, oftentimes that rapper, singer, etc. has been through life storms and the only way to seem normal, is to express themselves through their choice of language. Now the problem to that is influence. Who are you influencing and why? We must answer to God, not people necessarily.

I learned that life storms are necessary; and at times they can be very overwhelming and uncomfortable. However, during these storms; there's a breaking manifestation. There is a need of a higher power that working in and through us... that we tend to forget when we are working our own will. Jesus has taught me how to love him unconditional. He has taught increased through faith. He changed my carnal mind. I now do not want to become just for self-righteous gain; but to become resourceful to the nations. There are thousands of persons that I can relate. God allowed me to experience a tremendous amount, that I was unable to go into detail within this book; but know I'm ready. I could never get too comfortable in life; because I know for it to be true; "that" soon as you get too comfortable, you lose sight of God and now, you're on another roller coaster ride that's heading down hill fast

If there was one thing that I could say to someone with ears to hears; it would be: No matter where you are in life, never get too comfortable: follow by, find comfort in Jesus. Tell him your pains; because he's the ultimate help.

… pay close attention to the TOO. It's definitely okay to find comfort; but don't get too comfortable. That's not pleasing to the Father in Heaven; on earth; nor His only begotten son: Jesus Christ.

'If you're rich, don't get **too** comfortable.
If you are poor don't get **too** comfortable.
If you have an illness, don't get **too** comfortable.
If your considered healthy, don't get **too** comfortable.
If you can't have children, don't get **too** comfortable.
If you have children, don't get **too** comfortable.
If you're single, don't get **too** comfortable.
If you're married, don't get **too** comfortable.
If you want to die; don't get **too** comfortable.
If you lack understanding, guidance, and direction, don't get **too** comfortable.

If you're spiritual… don't get **too** comfortable. You too, can still get tricked by the enemy if not careful.

NO MATTER WHO YOU ARE; DON'T! GET! TOO! COMFORTABLE!!!!!

Body

The light of the body is the soul,

channeled by living water,

that you may never thirst again.

A Prayer for an Entrepreneurial Spirit, that's Defeating Generational Curses

Lord, since I know you're for me; help me to NOT do your job. Help to keep a heart of love, full of forgiveness. Keep me focused and available for your instructions. Thank you for helping me understand that obedience is better than sacrifice. Thank you for helping me understand Habakka; God you said in your word to write the vision and engrave it so plainly upon tablets that everyone who passes may be able to read it as easily and quickly as possible. Thank you, Father God, for giving me the courage and perseverance to exceed in entrepreneurship; taking entrepreneurship to executive positions in God-Class business; through your son Jesus Christ. God because of the purpose and plans you have for me: I know it's important to commune with you every day. You are ahead of my life. In you Lord Jesus is true love: peace, patience, kindness, goodness, faithfulness, gentleness, self-control, endurance, and understanding. Thank you, Lord, for preparing such persons for me that will help me meet your requirements for the Glory of Father God in Heaven. Thank you for allowing me to be experienced in failure. Thank you for teaching me how to trust you. Now Lord, as I die to self: I know you will do the impossible in my life. I stand today as a witness of how powerful and radiant you really are. Thanks for calling me your beloved. It's you I live for. It's you Lord Jesus that have created a newness in my being. I am no longer shackled to the generational cures that defined my brokenness. Lord, I thank you for sending Grace rainbow across and through my path. God it's your will that I want to orchestrate my business. God where there is a need; raise me up where I am able to pour; and never run empty. In Jesus Amen-

Live Remarks

Ayanna,

Uniquely created in a heavenly light.

Strong Black Queen, with a Lions fight. Heart full of love and joy. Be careful how you cross this one most of all. Blessed by the Best as far as east is from west. Solidified Butterfly going smoothly across this earth. Greatness is your Spirit, Excellence is your soul, Love is your heart after all. The Ambitious Eagle soars too high for anything to bring it down, always focused on goals at hand. The Soulful Saint and the virtuous woman run hand and hand sounds of a one accord symphony. – Tyrone

Ayanna Lea Tipton,

I pray that you continue to be the beacon of light that has time and time again led us away from the darkness. You are truly a gift from God. Thank you for being who you are!   ~ Sincerely, Dewon

Since the beginning, I knew she was different and the shining light of her flock. What a Lil lady; with some a big fight and heart. From trauma to triumph. This next journey of healing from speaking your truth and writing it down is the bravest thing ever! -Malcom

Mama's Boy Catering LLC.

Atlanta, Ga

Ayanna; known as Yanna aka Lil bit growing up. We definitely go way back to 48 school days. Walking up and down Carrollton and Guilford as kids. A person who is full of life, but so feisty lol literally laughed at any and everything. I'm blessed to be able to call you a friend. The love will be forever 🖤 beautiful person inside and out. I thank you for staying in touch. Your soul is so sweet and pure. Beautiful black queen forever and always. Naquesha Mayes

Ayanna Tipton aka Minjah was a Pretty Ballerina in High School at the Performing Arts School Formerly known as Broad Ripple High School for The Arts and Humanities located in Indianapolis Indiana. I've never known to not see a beautiful smile on her face, and Electric Energy Radiating through her little body. Truly an Angel. Wishing her Every single blessing God Has In Store for her life... Love Ya, ♥Mrs. Nicole Hargro

Performing Arts Dance Teacher/Company Director

I have known Ayanna since I was a freshman in High School at Ripple. She played a tremendous "Big Sister" role. Always supportive, loving, and caring. Beyond proud of all that you have and are going to continue to accomplish.

~Vae Savage

~WOLF

It started off as a high school crush. Always thinking of how I could get her attention more often, then I was worried about any schoolbooks. The issue used to be; we went to different schools; then the following semester she ended up at my school. I got to know her more as a caring, loving, and sincere individual... always with a smile on your face. Your smile could light even the darkest rooms. Now to see how much you have grown and developed just makes me so happy and all I see is the stars for you. Continue to elevate and Spread the love and happiness Ayanna. --

Ayanna Lea: STRENGTH!!!

Strength doesn't come from what you can do it comes from overcoming the things you thought you couldn't do. Ayanna Lea is a big example of how she pushes through everything. And when you look at her you will never know she is so passionate with everything she does. She helps restore people that have been through life trauma situations.

One thing I learn about life is you never know what tomorrow might bring. I was in a life-threatening car accident that changed me mentally as well as physically. But I am here today to let you know that we all have a purpose in life. Life has its ups, and we know life always has its downs but it's how we manage what's next in life. I now understand my purpose here on this earth, so I ask you, what is your purpose? ~PS. Martell Stott

Ayanna has been a very special person to me. She knows the right words to use and the right time. I pray God bless your work and Grant you everything your heart desires—

~Hakym Adegoke

Ayanna,

I wish you nothing but the best on your new journey. You have always been such an inspiration and light to me. Nothing is impossible for you. I pray that God continues to cover you and protect you. Always stay true to yourself. I'm proud of you. Love always, -Chels

Yanna,

Loving, strong, beautiful black queen. One thing I love is that you would give a person the shirt off yo back if they needed it. I remember u always lending a helping hand when needed, with no questions asked. Has a smile that could brighten up a room and a down to earth individual that wouldn't mind saying exactly what's on her mind, that's why we got along so well, never a dull moment, always good laughs. Despite the obstacles I know u faced u never gave up always pushed thru. ~Mashawn Joquin

Ayanna Lea: I had the pleasure of growing up with you and even when we were kids you always had something special about you. No matter what life threw at you, you're always pushing through it. God gives his strongest battles to his strongest people and boo you earned your stripes. There's always been a glow around you like a special Ora when you walk in rooms they light up and you my friend is the chosen one. Always remember you are loved. You can make it through, never give up and always put God first he will never leave you nor forsake you. I love you Ayanna and you made it, you are worthy, strong, intelligent, independent, and a beautiful black queen.   -Paris

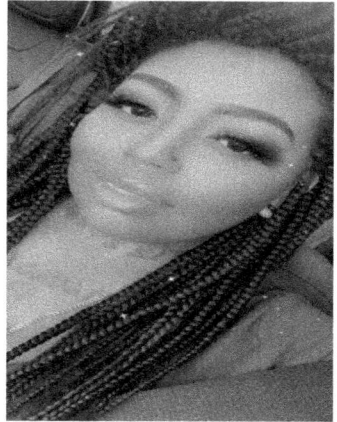

Ayanna has been a friend of mine since kindergarten. She is such a sweet, understanding, and outgoing person. I've watched her overcome tough barriers and blossom into an amazing author. I am so proud to call her my friend and I wish her nothing but positivity and success.

~Krecia Higgins

Ayanna,

I love the woman U Have Grown to Be.

You're Beautiful, Smart and Determined.

I wish u nothing but success in your life and Career; and

I have nothing but love for u. DEANDRE TRIPLET

Lance "Judah" Majors,

The best we have to offer the world is the reflection of love... You may or may not like what they see...but we get back what we put out... May your reflection be Ayanna –

A person with a heart of gold.
A person with a smile that glows.
A friend that never did me wrong
A friend that kept me standing strong
A queen that loves the skin she's in
A queen that would save the land
A woman in the best form
A woman who made it through the storm.
Ayanna, I appreciate you and all you do.
Keep up the good work. I'm proud of you. ~Big Meech

Ayanna,

You're an amazing person, friend, and mother. You deserve all that God has in store for you. May God continue to Bless you and all that your heart desires. Keep moving forward and blocking out the negativity and persevering. God won't put on you, more than you can bear. You got this. ~Jamila

I met Ayanna when I was a sophomore at Broad Ripple High School. She always looked very classy, always got heels and everything. I'm truly grateful for you.

-- Israel Gamble

Hey Gorgeous, I remember from school yu always had a warm, caring, fun, bubbly like personality. Overall, to me, yu were Beautiful inside and out..., but since school; I can't say I know you. I know you prayed 4us with our accident nd everything, nd I greatly appreciate yu 4dat

~Jazmin Hughley

Ayanna,

I pray that the door of blessings and success will continue to open for you. I pray to God that you keep your faith and to continue succeeding in every stage of life. I wish you good luck with the plans you have set. May God bless you! Congratulations and best wishes for your new adventures!   `Nae

Ayanna Lea,

You're such a beautiful soul. Your spirit is refreshing, and your laugh is contagious. Though you've been through hell and back, you're still standing tall. We've only known each other for a little while now, but I feel like this is a friendship that will last a lifetime. It's been a tremendous experience helping you bring your dream to life. "You Must Stand Out to Be Outstanding!" And Ayanna Lea- Outstanding you are. Much luck to you on your ventures. I can't wait to see where this journey takes you. I'll always be rooting for you Queen. -Much love, Jill

I am so proud of you Yanna, and all that you are becoming. I pray you'll forever and always get the blessings you deserve. You are one of the strongest people I know, and your resilience is incredible! No matter what comes your way you never give up and you made the best of it. You deserve everything and more. I love you- Egypt -

AYANNA, OVER THE YEARS YOU'VE GROWN AND
ACHIEVED SO MUCH IM SO PROUD OF YOU IN THE
YEARS OF GROWING IN OUR YOUNGER DAYS ALL WE
HAD WAS EACH OTHER WE HAD A HARD LIFE AND WE
CAME OUT TO BE
SUCCESSFUL WOMEN I HAVE
LEARNED SO MUCH FROM
YOU IN MY DARKEST DAYS
YOU WERE THERE TO GUIDE
ME THROUGH AND I THANK
YOU FOR THAT WE WILL
ALWAYS HAVE A SPECIAL
BOND AND I WANT YOU TO
CONTINUE TO ACCOMPLISH
AND CHASE YOUR DREAMS I LOVE YOU TO THE MOON
AND BACK ~SINCERELY KARINA

Ayanna Lea, I'm so lucky to have you
in my life. You motivate me and
encourage me to be a better version of
myself, I notice it and appreciate it so
very much. After getting to know you, I
never knew how much pain you were
experiencing because you always covered
your pain with a beautiful smile. Listening
to you and talking to you always
motivated me to be a better person and
you always encouraged me to keep my head up and move
forward no matter how hard life gets. You are so beautiful, and
I hope that everything continues to be nothing but greatness for
you ~Love always, Rhea

WHO ARE YOU:

JOY M. TORRENCE

Who are you? Who am I? Who, do we claim to be? You're from him? And from her? Oh so, now I see That your lineage, is who you are; Or who you choose to be: Or will you learn from their mistakes; and become whom God has called you to be. When will you learn your own worth? So, you can choose to be free,

To be free allows you to be you and me to be me Not worrying about the differences. OR holding on to any animosity. A growth within will only make you shine. Not that Gucci or that Prada or showing your bare behind. Stand tall and stand proud on who God says you are. Forget who the world has tried to make you. Remember you are a star. Hold that flame, be a light cuz your quality is within. A prodigy child born to win. For God sees you, You just have to let Him in. Who, are you? Who am I? Who, do we claim to be? You're from him? And from her? Oh, but now they will see that your past does not define you. When you choose to be free. Let God lead you, so you can be all that you are meant to be. ~ Joy M. Torrence

….. Who Am I, Ayanna Lea. Embracing all of me. Father God gets all the glory. Everyday, I have a heart of thanksgiving. I keep a heart of love: repentance.. and gratitude. I try my best to be the best version of me. I Am who, I Am because of I Am. No matter jealously… envy. Support or no support. I'm comfortable being me… Ayanna Lea.

Thankful for those who where able to speak life to me without any hidden agendas. I will never say.. I had no help; because help always came when I least excepted. I thank you all for being a part of my grooming and birthing. Thank you for showing me the light in myself that I couldn't meet. Love is never blind. I humbly that each one of you all.

Daddy, Thanks. Because without you…. I wouldn't be me.

Mommy, my rock. I thank you for being a vessel.

Aunts, Uncle, Cousins… thank you.

Best friends, friends, an associates… thank you.

Foes, haters… evil spirits… Thank you. Y'all really made a girl to a lady.

Rest in Peace Delise Michelle,

May Flower,
You got your flowers.
Holding, Pleasure Delight,
in the seeds of Leilani light.
Be still; and know that Jesus raced your night.
May flower, more like lasting Days in Flowers,
May Flower. I'll miss you. I'm never saying goodbye,
but hey flower. Leilani Delise is Heavenly flowers,
covering the fields with color for a mother.

Sunrise: May 26th
Sunset: March 9th of 2021
56 Strong

Sunrise

Breath took a rest. In the days that troubled the best.. God
commanded rest; the best stage of peace met. Memories we hold;
even the bad… We now look, smile, and be glad. I couldn't picture
life with losing you. Death had to be, so peace could sleep. To
sunrise; the crack of dawn graced morning dew. In the day we'll rise;
Sunrise lifted in the color of rainbows, gracing the sky: Sunrise… we
love sweet bliss of color, promising peace. Sunrise put away the heat.
Sunrise; set where peace met

Follow me on my Journey to the Promised Land.
The end is the start of a new beginning.

Minjah Gra

Makings Dreams a Reality.

M95: Ayanna Lea

www.ingramcontent.com/pod-product-compliance
Lightning Source LLC
Chambersburg PA
CBHW051843090426
42736CB00011B/1933